Practical
Innovation
in Government

Practical
Innovation
in Government

HOW FRONT-LINE LEADERS
ARE TRANSFORMING
PUBLIC-SECTOR ORGANIZATIONS

ALAN G. ROBINSON and DEAN M. SCHROEDER

BK®

Berrett–Koehler Publishers, Inc.

Berrett-Koehler Publishers, Inc.
1333 Broadway, Suite 1000
Oakland, CA 94612-1921
Tel: (510) 817-2277
Fax: (510) 817-2278
www.bkconnection.com

ORDERING INFORMATION

Quantity sales. Special discounts are available on quantity purchases by corporations, associations, and others. For details, contact the "Special Sales Department" at the Berrett-Koehler address above.

Individual sales. Berrett-Koehler publications are available through most bookstores. They can also be ordered directly from Berrett-Koehler: Tel: (800) 929-2929; Fax: (802) 864-7626; www.bkconnection.com.

Orders for college textbook / course adoption use. Please contact Berrett-Koehler: Tel: (800) 929-2929; Fax: (802) 864-7626.

Distributed to the U.S. trade and internationally by Penguin Random House Publisher Services.

Berrett-Koehler and the BK logo are registered trademarks of Berrett-Koehler Publishers, Inc.

Printed in the United States of America

Berrett-Koehler books are printed on long-lasting acid-free paper. When it is available, we choose paper that has been manufactured by environmentally responsible processes. These may include using trees grown in sustainable forests, incorporating recycled paper, minimizing chlorine in bleaching, or recycling the energy produced at the paper mill.

Library of Congress Cataloging-in-Publication Data
Names: Robinson, Alan (Alan G.), author. | Schroeder, Dean M., author.
Title: Practical innovation in government : how front-line leaders are transforming public-sector organizations / Alan G. Robinson and Dean M. Schroeder.
Description: First edition. | Oakland, CA : Berrett-Koehler Publishers, 2022. | Includes bibliographical references and index.
Identifiers: LCCN 2021057345 (print) | LCCN 2021057346 (ebook) | ISBN 9781523001781 (hardcover) | ISBN 9781523001798 (pdf) | ISBN 9781523001804 (epub)
Subjects: LCSH: Administrative agencies--Reorganization. | Organizational change. | Government productivity.
Classification: LCC JF1525.O73 R63 2022 (print) | LCC JF1525.O73 (ebook) | DDC 352.3/67--dc23/eng/20220204
LC record available at https://lccn.loc.gov/2021057345
LC ebook record available at https://lccn.loc.gov/2021057346

First Edition
27 26 25 24 23 22   10 9 8 7 6 5 4 3 2 1

Book producer and text designer: Maureen Forys, Happenstance Type-O-Rama
Cover designer: Kim Scott/Bumpy Design

To the people on the front lines of our
public-sector organizations.
With their creativity and ideas,
we can transform government operations.

CONTENTS

PART 4   WHEN GOVERNMENT LEADS THE WAY: PUSHING THE BOUNDARIES OF INNOVATION AND IMPROVEMENT

PREFACE

We never set out to write a book about improving government operations. We were drawn in slowly as we learned more and as the potential of what we were discovering became increasingly apparent. Throughout our careers, our work has centered on high-performance organizations. Until recently this meant that we studied and worked primarily with private-sector companies.

But a few years ago, we became aware of some impressive improvement efforts in public-sector organizations. Fascinated, we started to visit them and look into what they were doing. Gradually, as we identified and visited more such organizations, it became clear that the highest performers were using approaches that, although rare in the private sector, were proving astonishingly effective in a government setting. In fact, some of these organizations had attained levels of efficiency and service that rivalled the best private-sector companies anywhere.

For decades, most books on improving government operations have assumed that the only way to do this is to make sweeping changes, such as dismantling bureaucracy, privatizing services, reengineering budgeting and purchasing processes, or eliminating cumbersome rules and policies. Underlying this line of thinking is that in order to be more efficient, government needs to be run more like a business. Unfortunately, this approach merely replaces old problems with new ones.

What we discovered in our research was compelling. The organizations we studied had dramatically improved their performance *within existing government constraints.* In other words, their methods accepted government on its own terms, with its needed checks and balances, its complex public mission, its inherent political character, its diverse stakeholder demands, and with its operating goals that transcend narrow financial concerns. And the interest in improvement came from across the political spectrum—there was *no* pattern associating the improvement initiatives with any particular political orientation. What we were seeing was practical innovation in government.

In the beginning, we had expected to find that successful improvement and innovation efforts in the public sector would look very much like they did in well-run private-sector companies, perhaps with some contextual adjustments. But we found these initiatives using a fundamentally different approach, and it was a game-changer. Rather than most improvement efforts being driven by middle and upper managers, as is typical in the private sector, the primary champions of change in the high-performing government organizations were low-level managers and front-line employees.

As we learned more, what had begun as a personal curiosity turned into a book that simply had to be written. Written for front-line supervisors and managers interested in dramatically improving the performance of their units by creating an engaged workforce. Written for higher-level government managers and elected officials looking for a practical way to transform the operations of a large department, a city, or even an entire state. Written for the professionals, senior staff, and thinkers about government who have the ear of public-sector leaders and managers. And finally, written for students of public administration, who are the future of government.

The book's stories and insights are drawn from extensive field research and interviews with people at all levels of the organizations we studied. Our goal is to demonstrate the enormous potential of front-line–driven improvement for you and your organization, to inspire you to try it yourself, and to provide you with a well-grounded and realistic guide to help you succeed in improving your own part of government.

We hope you find *Practical Innovation in Government* both useful and enjoyable.

INTRODUCTION
The Practical Secret to High-Performing Government Operations

Whether people want more government or less government, they all want *efficient* government. Unfortunately, public-sector organizations are generally not known for their operational excellence. Recently, however, a small but growing number of public-sector organizations around the world have demonstrated that it is possible to dramatically improve performance in a government setting. We spent six years studying improvement efforts in over seventy government organizations—ranging from small departments to entire states—in five countries. Some were struggling or had already failed. Others were just getting started or had made limited progress in specific areas. But a handful of high performers had developed truly world-class levels of efficiency and service. Our intent was to discover how these high performers had succeeded in transforming themselves when so much of government has not.

To get a sense for the kind of transformation we will be talking about, consider what happened in the Department of Excise and Licenses in the city of Denver.

On a hot August day, Stacie Loucks walked into the department and immediately knew she had her work cut out for her. The waiting area was crammed with hot and irritated customers, so many that the air conditioning system could not get the temperature below eighty-five degrees. Loucks had just been appointed by Mayor Michael Hancock to head the department, whose thirty-nine employees issued some forty-eight thousand licenses each year. The approximately eighty different types of licenses, most of which required annual renewals, included everything from individual licenses for taxi drivers and merchant (security) guards to business licenses for restaurants and liquor stores.

Loucks knew that if nothing was done, the long waits were going to get much worse. The city's booming economy meant that the number of business licenses being issued was expected to double in the next three years. Furthermore, voters had recently legalized the recreational use of marijuana, and the city was going to have to figure out how to license all aspects of its growth, testing, distribution, and sales. And since Colorado was the first state to legalize recreational marijuana, there were no models to follow. There was also talk of developing licensing requirements for short-term private lodging rentals (think Airbnb), and for drivers working for ridesharing companies such as Uber and Lyft.

Fortunately, Loucks had a place to go for help. She called Brian Elms, Director of Peak Academy, the city's continuous improvement office. He assigned one of his improvement experts, Melissa Wiley, to the department for six months to help Loucks get things started.

Although the problem seemed obvious, Wiley quickly discovered that no one had any data on actual wait times, nor had specific causes of the delays been identified. Consequently, her first action was to set up a system to measure and track various aspects of the service process in order to better understand the issues involved. It turned out that the average wait time to see a license technician was one hour and forty minutes, with peak times of over five hours.

While Wiley was gathering data, Loucks began to mobilize her unit for a serious improvement effort. Over the next eighteen months, she and her employees came up with many improvement ideas, most of which they could implement themselves. Wait times for licenses were cut to seven minutes, and peak wait times to less than fifteen minutes. As the staff were no longer serving hostile customers who had been waiting for hours, their work became less stressful and unpleasant. Morale increased and employee turnover declined dramatically. And despite the dramatic increase in license volume, Loucks was the only department head in the entire city government who did not ask for more staff or resources in the next budgeting cycle.

On a follow-up visit to Denver Licensing several years later, the first thing we noticed was that *no one* was waiting to be served. And as we shall see, the reduction in wait times was only the beginning of the department's transformation.

Rethinking Improvement in Government Operations

There is a long history of attempts to eliminate waste in the public sector. Over the years, a number of prominent national-level commissions have recommended sweeping reorganizations and dramatic policy changes aimed at streamlining operations and saving money. (More on these in the next chapter.) Although these one-off efforts did make some progress, they fell far short of what was possible.

Countless initiatives in state and local governments have attempted to create some form of ongoing improvement capability, typically drawing on the popular improvement methodologies of the day.[1] Unfortunately, most of these programs produced only limited results. They rarely succeeded in creating the culture and systems needed to engage employees at all levels in sustained and broad-based *continuous* improvement (CI).

Throughout our careers, our main interest has been operational improvement. We have studied its history, and have even been drawn into our own historical studies, conducting direct archival research on topics ranging from the earliest suggestion systems at the Arsenal in medieval Venice to the emergence of what would become the modern CI movement during and after WWII in the United States and Japan. We studied best practices wherever we could find them in the world and brought much of what we learned to our corporate clients who were seeking to upgrade their own CI efforts. Our primary goal was to learn more about the facets of leadership and organizational structure that energize, or retard, ongoing performance improvement. And the field of CI has never stopped evolving and expanding into new areas.

Most of our work has been in the private sector, where interest in operational improvement has always been strong. But several years ago, we experienced a marked increase of interest in our research and consulting help from government managers. They were dissatisfied with the results of their CI initiatives and wanted to know how to do better. We had previously worked with CI efforts in public-sector organizations, but we had often left thinking that our efforts should have had more impact than they did. Clearly, we were missing something.

The renewed interest in CI started us thinking. Neither of us was aware of any public-sector CI initiatives that came anywhere near the high-performing ones we had studied or worked with in the private sector. Was there something different about government organizations that made CI more challenging for them?

We began searching for examples of public-sector organizations with good CI programs, seeking help from academic colleagues, friends in the government consulting world, and our contacts in government. Early on, many of the programs we visited were marginal or in their early stages. Gradually, we began to find more organizations with strong improvement cultures. Ultimately, as we mentioned, we studied over seventy organizations in five countries. Of these, we classified fifteen as exceptionally high performers, with work environments like Denver Licensing, where fully engaged employees were regularly solving problems and making improvements. A handful of these high performers were operating at levels of efficiency and service on a par with the best companies we had seen in the private sector.

> The high-performing public-sector organizations were operating at levels of efficiency and service that rivalled the best private-sector companies anywhere.

In hindsight, the reason for the initial scarcity of effective programs was that we had begun our search just as a new generation of improvement initiatives was emerging. Many of the high-performing initiatives described in this book were still in their early stages, and several did not yet exist. Our fortuitous timing offered a rare opportunity to study the development of these programs as they grew from their earliest stages into instruments of transformative change. We interviewed over a thousand people, from front-line staff to top political leaders, and compared the characteristics of our sample of high-performing programs with those that were limping along or delivering limited results. Our goal was to discover the success factors for CI in government and to understand their implications for managers at all levels. Our methodology was loosely what academics would refer to as a "grounded theory" approach—probing, testing, and refining our thinking with each new interview or case.

The high performers were achieving their impressive levels of efficiency and service in a surprising way. We had expected to find most improvement being driven in a top-down fashion, perhaps by middle or upper managers, as is generally the case in the business world. Although we did find plenty of examples of management-driven programs, they were the marginal and low performers—their performance was spotty and their lifespans were often short. Some were so short-lived that we were unable to study them directly. Much of our information about them came from postmortems. We found ourselves interviewing, and commiserating with, the people involved after their programs had been terminated.

The successful CI efforts we studied were quite different. What stood out was that the lion's share of the improvement activity was taking place on the front lines. The primary champions of change were low-level managers and supervisors. They had created units with strong local cultures of improvement. Bit by bit, through large numbers of small, highly targeted ideas, their units relentlessly increased performance. These *front-line leaders*, not their higher-level managers, were the real heroes of their organizations' innovation stories.

The more we studied this front-line–driven improvement, the more we realized how uniquely suited it is to a government context. This book distills the collective experiences of the leaders we studied and the lessons they learned. Our goal is to lay out what is different about CI in public-sector organizations—what *works*, what *doesn't*, and *why*.

But before we get into our findings, it will be helpful to get a better understanding of what front-line–driven improvement actually looks like. To do this, let us take a closer look at what Stacie Loucks did to transform Denver Licensing.

Transformative Improvement at Denver Licensing

When Loucks took over as department head, one of the first things she needed to do was to figure out why the lines were so long. So she asked Melissa Wiley (the expert loaned to her from Peak Academy) to dissect and measure the different aspects of the problem. In the process, Wiley discovered some startling contributing factors. A huge one was the fact that 40 percent of the people who finally made it to the service counter were turned away because their applications were incomplete or they had filled out the wrong forms. Each license typically required five to eight different forms, and it was easy to confuse them or miss one entirely. The applicants would then have to leave the line, get the correct documentation, and in many cases, get in line all over again.

While Wiley was busy analyzing the long lines, Loucks was looking for ways to free up some time for her overwhelmed service technicians to participate in improvement activity. She scheduled a meeting with the city's budget director to get permission to convert two open (but unneeded) "enforcement officer" positions into licensing technician positions. On her way to the meeting, she received a text from Wiley informing her that the wait time had just reached eight hours! Armed with this additional information, Loucks had little difficulty convincing the budget director to allow her to convert the positions.

As soon as she could, Loucks began sending her entire staff of thirty-nine people to Peak Academy for training. Over several months, her front-line employees were given "green belt" training, a one-day workshop on the basic tools of CI, and her supervisors and managers received a more extensive five-day "black belt" course.

To encourage front-line staff to put their training to use as soon as they got back to the office, Loucks asked each employee to identify at least one improvement by the end of the year, then several months away. The improvement had to help reduce customer wait times and be one that the employee could implement without a great deal of help. As an additional spur, these ideas would be taken into account in the employees' annual performance reviews.

Most of the ideas involved relatively small changes that were simple to implement. For example,

- A licensing technician came up with an idea to address the problem of applicants who filled out the wrong forms. This mistake was easy to make, because a lot of the forms looked similar and applications typically required five to eight different forms, many of which were used for several different licenses. The merchant guard license application, for example, required an application form, a letter of hire, a medical history form, a criminal history form, a criminal background check, copies of photo-identification documents, and three character references. One day an applicant for this license came in with a nicely organized packet of forms. When the technician complemented him on his organizational skills, he remarked that the packet was simply the way his new boss had handed him the forms. Thinking about this, the technician realized that while all the necessary forms were available in the lobby, they were organized by form, rather than by license. This meant that the applicants had to assemble the correct set of forms for whatever license they were seeking. The technician decided to create preassembled packets of forms for the five most popular licenses. As a result, for these licenses the problem of applicants filling out the incorrect forms was eliminated.

■ The office had a single centralized printer/copier/scanner for everyone's use. This arrangement was intended to save money and space, but it meant that whenever technicians had to print a document, make a copy, or scan an applicant's ID or other documentation, they would have to get up, leave their customer, and walk across the office to the shared machine. And with the entire office using the machine, there was often a queue. To eliminate this wasted time, a technician suggested equipping each customer service counter with its own desktop printer/copier/scanner. After a quick analysis, Loucks ordered the printers.

■ A computer and printer had been set up in the lobby so that applicants needing to submit criminal background checks could conduct and print these checks themselves. The problem was that the specialized software was not user-friendly. Customers were constantly getting stuck and having to ask a licensing technician for help. On average this happened thirty-six times a day, with each incident taking about five minutes of a technician's time. The improvement idea was to create a simple instruction manual with screen shots and arrows to walk applicants through the process step by step. It saved three hours in technician time per day.

■ When applicants submitted their forms, the technicians had to enter their information into the computer. The problem was that the input screens were set up differently than the forms, requiring technicians to constantly flip pages back and forth to locate the right information. Not only was this irritating and time-consuming, but it led to input errors. A technician suggested that the application forms be redesigned to match the computer screens.

While most front-line ideas could be handled with little or no help from managers, occasionally a larger idea came up that needed Loucks's involvement. For example, a license technician proposed that the department digitize its licensing records. Historically, license records had been kept on paper and filed in boxes on shelves. When a file was needed by a licensing technician or requested by someone in another city department, such as a police officer checking into a business, it would take a technician ten to fifteen minutes of searching to retrieve it—if the file was where it was supposed to be. If the record had been misfiled or taken out by someone else, the technician would usually abandon the search after thirty minutes or so and send out an all-office email to try to locate it. Retrieving records was a major source of delay and frustration.

The more we studied front-line–driven improvement, the more we realized how uniquely suited it is to a government context.

Loucks procured the equipment and IT support the employee needed for the digitalization process, and she also freed time for her and a colleague to work through the files. Over the next several months, as time was available, the pair culled old documents according to the city's document retention protocol and digitized the rest. The digitization project not only eliminated a lot of wasted time searching for files, but it made license information available online to any city employee who needed it. The project also freed up a large area in the center of the main office where the paper files had been stored.

A number of other significant problems also required Loucks's personal involvement. Early on, to check on how telephone inquiries were being handled, Loucks called the public phone number for Denver Licensing. Her call was not answered, and the voice mailbox was full. By accessing the mailbox and listening to some of the messages, Loucks discovered that many people were calling with simple questions and then calling back two or three times after getting no response. Eventually, they were forced to come in and join the line in the service center. It turned out that although the staff was aware of the voice mailbox, no one had responsibility to check it and return calls. Loucks had no data on how many calls had been received, but she did discover fourteen thousand open inquiries that had been forwarded to her department from calls made to 311, Denver's non-emergency phone number. She realized that the ignored phone calls were contributing to the long wait times.

Loucks discussed the problem with the head of the city's 311 service, who was under some pressure to improve his unit's first-call resolution rate, and he was eager to work with her. Together, he and Loucks developed a list of answers to frequently asked questions (FAQs) and incorporated it into a short training session for the city's 311 operators. This allowed them to answer approximately half of the questions about licenses, and it gave a big boost to their first-call resolution rate. Loucks also established a standard procedure to manage the voice mailbox, creating a schedule for service technicians to review messages and respond to them.

As we mentioned earlier, within eighteen months, wait times at Denver Licensing dropped from an average of one hour and forty minutes to seven minutes. Peak wait times dropped from over five hours to fifteen minutes. And not long afterward, wait times were all but eliminated.

As soon as the wait-time problem was solved, Loucks turned her department's CI focus to streamlining the service experience once customers got to the technicians. And when Loucks's successor, Ashley Kilroy, stepped into the leadership role without the pressure of the long lines and service issues, she and the staff were able to take on higher-order issues and challenge some longstanding norms. They worked with the mayor and city council to reexamine a number of the licensing rules. The application processes for many licenses were put online, and the need for several other licenses was eliminated. For example, taxi drivers required licenses, but ridesharing drivers did not. Naturally, the taxi drivers were upset. After some study and discussion, rather than adding the requirement that rideshare drivers be licensed, the licensing requirements for taxi drivers were reduced.

The Emergence of the Front-Line Leader

Loucks's success in dramatically improving performance at Denver Licensing required a great deal of leadership on her part. She had to plan the change, inspire her staff to get involved in improvement activity, create the time to get them trained, secure help from Peak Academy and permission from the city's budget office, and then lead her people through the actual transformation effort. All the high-performing programs we studied were characterized by such extraordinary leadership at the front-line level.

In most organizations, the lower managers are in the hierarchy, the less they need to demonstrate leadership. Their primary tasks are to coordinate, supervise, direct, and control, based on procedures and policies established by managers higher up the chain of command. Building a unit driven by front-line improvement requires more leadership at a lower level than is the norm.

A strong front-line–driven CI component turned out to be the primary difference between successful CI initiatives in public-sector organizations and those in their private-sector counterparts. It took us a while to figure out why.

The Challenges of Management-Driven Improvement in Government

It seems obvious: most improvement must be driven by top and middle managers. After all, they are the ones with authority and access to resources. And management-driven CI is indeed the dominant paradigm in the private sector. So why did our study find it delivering such limited results in government, and why was most of the effective improvement activity taking place on the front lines?

In the private sector, changes are generally less complicated to execute. If top or middle managers want to make a change, they usually have the power to do so. But government is not a business. When government managers want to create change, they typically face a host of political, regulatory, and bureaucratic hurdles that can make the process painfully slow, inordinately time consuming, and even professionally risky.

> Building a front-line–driven unit requires
> substantially more leadership from lower-level
> managers and supervisors than is the norm.

Public-sector organizations have many checks and balances. Some are in the form of divided authority, but most are embedded in policies and rules that were put in place to ensure consistency, fairness, openness, due process, or ethical behavior. Over time, successive managers add their own interpretations to these policies and rules, and these interpretations can gradually become considered part of the policies and rules as well. The result is that managers trying to make even modest improvements must contend with a bureaucratic haze of uncertainty in which it is not always clear what is allowable. All this makes it more complex and riskier for them to make changes.

Harry Kenworthy, a consultant who conducted many Rapid Improvement Events (RIEs) in the public sector (more on RIEs in Chapter 9), used to insist that before a team he was working with started one, it should examine all the policies and rules that might get in the way of any potential changes. The CI department of one Midwestern state we studied had a team of five lawyers attached to it whose primary task was to make sure that improvements did not violate any existing laws or regulations. Their secondary task was to convince the legislature to modify specific laws in ways that would allow increases in efficiency while not impacting the laws' intent.

In addition, most management-driven improvements are large enough to have budget implications. The public-sector budgeting process often involves political wrangling, horse-trading, and compromise in a zero-sum game where constituencies with different agendas vie for limited resources. Funding an improvement project often means not funding something else.

Another factor is the nature of top leadership in government. As the city manager of Borås, a community in Southwest Sweden noted for its CI initiative, pointed out to us, "Democratic government is one of the few places where the leaders generally know far less about how their organizations work than the people who report to them." This can make management-driven change challenging. When managers propose an improvement that needs top-level support, they often find themselves trying to make their case to leaders who lack the background and contextual understanding needed to make an informed decision. And when elected officials start imposing "improvements" themselves, the results can be extremely disruptive.

One local Canadian school official told us that every time a new Provincial education minister takes office, the central ministry sends out a new set of educational "experts" to introduce the latest teaching "innovations" to her schools and teachers. Since these outsiders have little understanding of local realities, their "improvements" invariably create more problems than they solve.

Given the unique challenges faced by management-driven improvement in the public sector, CI initiatives designed around it are hobbled from the outset. Front-line–driven improvement, however, largely avoids these drawbacks. Moreover, it is an unexpectedly powerful force for change.

Why Front-Line–Driven Improvement Is So Effective

Although the front-line ideas implemented at Denver Licensing were generally small and inexpensive, cumulatively they all but eliminated the long lines. At the same time, each individual idea went largely unnoticed by customers, colleagues from other departments, and higher-level managers. In short, they were invisible to outsiders. And even if outsiders had become aware of one of these ideas, where would any potential objection to it have come from?

Without the countervailing forces faced by higher-level managers, front-line leaders and staff can implement large numbers of small improvements with little interference. And when ideas do need to involve other functions, front-line leaders can often work directly with their counterparts in other departments—much as Loucks did with her 311 colleague.

In spite of being so small that they are "under the radar," front-line ideas are an amazingly powerful source of improvement. Research has shown that some 80 percent of any organization's improvement potential lies in the creativity and initiative of its front-line staff.[2] (The other 20 percent comes from the ideas of consultants and managers, new technology, improved equipment, etc.) We have come to call this phenomenon "The 80/20 Principle of Improvement." There are many reasons behind it. For one thing, front-line staff are in positions to see a lot of problems that their managers do not and, as we saw in the Denver Licensing examples, they have intimate, process-specific knowledge that allows them to come up with practical, low-cost improvements. There are also a lot more front-line employees than managers.

> Despite being so small that they are "under the radar," front-line ideas are an amazingly powerful source of improvement. Front-line leaders and staff are able to implement large numbers of them with little interference.

Additionally, many "small" front-line ideas are much bigger than their apparent "face value," because they apply to activities that are repeated, sometimes thousands or even tens of thousands of times a year. Take, for example, the case of Denver Licensing's clearer manual for applicants generating their own background checks. The new manual saved the technicians some 36 interruptions per day, or more than 9,300 interruptions per year. At 5 minutes per interruption, this translated to 3 hours per day, which is 15 hours per week, or 750 hours per year. And this was just a single idea! With the sheer quantity of ideas that front-line–driven improvement can generate, the benefits quickly accumulate into astonishing performance improvement. But no one, even the front-line employees themselves, ever sees the full impact of individual ideas. Each small idea quickly disappears into normal work routines and is forgotten. All anyone sees is a well-run department.

Given the near invisibility of individual front-line ideas, it is not surprising that so many managers are unaware of the 80/20 Principle of Improvement. And even when it is explained to them, many simply don't believe it. We remember being challenged when introducing the concept during a training session at a large US Naval base. When we brought up the 80/20 Principle, one of the improvement experts taking the class abruptly got up and left the room. He returned a while later and apologized. Not believing us, he had gone to run the numbers to refute our point. He had realized that the improvement data kept by the base could be separated by source—management or the front lines. But the results of his analysis confirmed that almost exactly 80 percent of the overall improvement that had taken place on the base in the previous year had been front-line initiated!

When it became clear to us that the dominant factor distinguishing the high performers in our study was front-line–driven improvement, we were surprised, yet not surprised. Surprised, because we were simply not expecting to see its singular importance in the government context. Not surprised, because in the relatively few cases of true front-line–driven improvement in the private sector, it also produces extremely high rates of performance improvement.

Organization-Wide Front-Line–Driven Improvement

Part 1 of this book is designed to provide front-line managers with what they need to know to create a front-line–driven unit, much of which is counterintuitive. Part 2—Chapters 5 to 7—shifts the perspective to higher-level leaders who want to deploy front-line–driven improvement across a large department, city, state, or national-level agency.

We identified and tracked eight successful organization-wide CI initiatives, observing the strategies the leaders used to transform their organizations and how each strategy played out.

The successful strategies all followed a similar pattern. The top leaders began by working to convince their senior leadership teams of the benefits of front-line–driven improvement. Once they felt that there was an adequate level of support for the concept, the leaders began installing the instruments of change in their organizations. They started by appointing someone to lead the transformation— someone with deep CI expertise, solid change-management skills, and a good measure of institutional intelligence.

These CI champions were responsible for designing and setting up the infrastructure needed for the improvement initiative. Their first step was to assemble a small group of experts who could act as trainers, coaches, and facilitators during the rollout and ongoing development of CI throughout the organization.

To launch their CI initiatives, many of the leaders used some version of what Denver's Brian Elms termed "building a coalition of the willing." Rather than wasting their efforts on reluctant managers, the leaders invested time and resources only in the managers who already wanted to get involved. This is markedly different from how CI initiatives are typically launched in the private sector, where top management simply mandates participation. While dictating the use of CI can generate rapid compliance and gets the initiative off to a fast start, it also tends to generate resentment rather than the high levels of engagement needed for front-line–driven improvement. Engagement does not come from conscripts; it comes from *volunteers*.

Engagement does not come from conscripts;
it comes from volunteers.

Over time, as evidence of the benefits of front-line–driven improvement mounts, the coalition of the willing expands as more managers become convinced of its merits. And as CI becomes more accepted, the leaders begin ratcheting up accountability for it by including improvement performance in annual reviews and decisions on raises and promotions.

Improvement in the Interconnected World of Problems and Opportunities

Every organization faces a spectrum of problems and opportunities. These come in different sizes and complexities, need to be addressed at different levels of analysis, and are often part of an interrelated nesting of issues. The effective CI programs in our study assembled a complete set of problem-solving techniques that could address the range and types of issues their organizations typically encountered. In Part 3—Chapters 8 through 11—we discuss the three main categories of problems and some of the more frequently used methods to deal with them.

Our goal is not to teach or advocate for any particular technique. Many books, classes, consultants, and online resources are available to help with that. Rather, we introduce and describe the power of various problem-solving methods, demonstrate why a full set of them is needed, and use numerous stories to illustrate them. For example, we show how

- the front-line idea system at the Colorado Department of Transportation (CDOT) significantly increased productivity, reduced costs, improved the road system, and made the highway crews' jobs easier and much safer;

- a Rapid Improvement Event (RIE) in the city of Denton, Texas, cut 25 days out of its hiring process and saved 688 staff hours per year;

- a K–8 school in New Brunswick, Canada, used Lean Six Sigma to boost the percentage of students reading at the appropriate age level from 22 percent to 78 percent; and

- the State of Washington used the A3 process to deal with a very complex and politically charged problem involving twenty-four state and federal agencies, as well as four Native American tribes.

We end our discussion of CI methods with a description of the system at the Royal Mint, whose full spectrum of improvement tools (including several clever techniques developed in-house) have made it highly efficient and capable of minting the most difficult coins in the world to counterfeit.

Innovative Approaches to Improvement in the Public Sector

The first three parts of this book explain how an increasing number of public-sector organizations are attaining very high performance, mostly by borrowing CI concepts developed in the private sector. The fourth and final part—Chapters 12 through 15—reverses this pattern. It describes how a handful of innovative government organizations are pushing the boundaries of CI in ways that even the best private-sector companies could learn from.

> Some of the organizations in our study had pioneered some innovative approaches to CI that even the best-managed private-sector companies could learn from.

We describe how

- the York Region of Ontario, Canada, developed creative approaches to engage large numbers of front-line staff in solving problems that are normally the exclusive domain of management;

- Highways England, the authority responsible for all major motorways in England, created an innovative supply chain and saved hundreds of millions of pounds;

- the city of Denver, the first major US city to legalize recreational marijuana, developed a fast-reaction CI system to respond to the highly fluid, rapidly emerging, and potentially dangerous cannabis ecosystem; and

- Denmark's MindLab, its governmental innovation unit, pioneered a process to expose high-level policymakers to front-line realities and help them create much more effective laws and policies.

A Final Note

Armed with the right knowledge and mindset, we believe that almost any manager, including a front-line supervisor, can create a local culture of highly engaged employees who are constantly improving their unit's performance. It requires persistence, and it will not happen overnight. For those who choose to make their part of government better, we hope the lessons we were able to distill from the successful leaders in our study will prove invaluable.

PART 1

Front-Line–Driven Improvement

The successful leaders in our study did not rely exclusively on management-driven improvement to transform their organizations. Most of the change came through large numbers of modest improvements made at the front-line level. Part 1 of this book makes the case for front-line–driven improvement and shows how the front-line leaders we studied made it happen.

Chapter 1 explains why large high-level and management-driven change initiatives have had such limited success in a public-sector context. Chapter 2 discusses how seemingly small front-line ideas, whose importance is generally over-looked by managers, have a surprisingly large impact. Chapter 3 examines the practices and behaviors of effective front-line leaders, as well as the role these play in creating a local front-line improvement culture. Chapter 4 lays out the key leverage points in the process of transforming an ordinary unit into one that is front-line driven.

Front-line–driven change is surprisingly powerful. Perhaps more important, it is a practical approach to innovation and improvement that is particularly well suited to government organizations.

1

The Problems with Management-Driven Improvement in Government

We did not expect to find that the most successful transformations of government operations in our study would be characterized by front-line–driven improvement. Like so many others who have worked with continuous improvement (CI) in the public-sector, we were unwittingly working under two assumptions, both wrong. First, radical performance improvement in government must be driven by high-level leadership, whether elected or administrative. Second, the same approaches used in the business world will work in government too. But government is not a business, and what works for CI in the private sector does not always work as well in the public sector. We were surprised when we figured out why.

The Limitations of Top-Driven Improvement

When we talk with people about improving efficiency in government, they often bring up one of the handful of high-profile national government initiatives that have taken place over the last century.

These initiatives had bold goals and visionary agendas, and they held out the prospect of major change.

One of the more successful high-level initiatives to promote government efficiency in the United States was the Commission on Organization of the Executive Branch of the Government, more commonly known as the Hoover Commission. Established by President Truman shortly after WWII, its purpose was to realign government from a wartime to a peacetime configuration by consolidating federal government departments in order to eliminate duplication of services. Truman appointed ex-President Hoover to head the nonpartisan commission, which had equal representation of Democrats and Republicans. Hoover had a reputation as a reformer from his leadership of the "War on Waste" shortly after WWI, while he was Secretary of Commerce in President Coolidge's administration. The Hoover Commission ran from 1947 to 1949, and was reestablished from 1953 to 1955 by President Eisenhower, to address concerns over the rapid growth in the size of government during the Korean War. The two commissions offered a total of 587 recommendations, more than 70 percent of which were implemented through a combination of administrative action and congressional legislation.[1] Some of the notable outcomes of the commission's work included the formation of both the Department of Health, Education, and Welfare (HEW) and the General Services Administration (GSA), as well as the modernization of the federal budgeting process.

Another prominent national effort to eliminate waste in government was initiated in 1982 by President Reagan. He created the Private Sector Survey on Cost Control (PSSCC), popularly known as the Grace Commission after its head, J. Peter Grace, CEO of W.R. Grace and Company. The commission's charge, as Reagan famously put it, was to "drain the swamp." Its final report contained hundreds of detailed examples of government waste (many of which are listed in the book *Burning Money* that Grace published later[2]). The report estimated that its nearly 2,500 recommendations would generate more than $424 billion in savings in just the first three years after their

implementation.[3] Congress ignored all the policy-related recommendations, but a few of the specific examples of waste identified by the
commission were acted upon.

In March 1993, President Clinton asked Vice President Gore to
lead the National Performance Review (NPR), an interagency task
force whose goal was to streamline the Federal government. (In
1998, the NPR was renamed the National Partnership for Reinventing Government.) The NPR's two-thousand-page report with 383 recommendations claimed that $108 billion could be saved through less
bureaucracy, reducing overhead, program changes, and streamlining the contracting process.[4] Just like Reagan's initiative, its ambitious
agenda of reform and improvement ran into strong political head-
winds, and relatively few of its recommendations were implemented.

A more recent national-level initiative to transform government
took place in Britain under Prime Minister Tony Blair. While he ran
for a second term, his campaign message focused on improving the
areas of education, health, crime, and transportation. Shortly after
being reelected in May 2001, Blair created the Prime Minister's Delivery Unit—which adopted the Deliverology approach developed by
Sir Michael Barber, its first head—to follow through on his campaign
promises. Although it did achieve most of its goals, most notably on
the childhood education front, the Delivery Unit was abolished by
the coalition government in 2010, after Blair resigned from office.

Such high-level initiatives—whether at the national, state, or city
level—are important for big-picture moves, such as restructuring
agencies and making major policy changes. But they cannot do much
to improve day-to-day operational efficiency. They are not capable of
penetrating the multiple layers of the government hierarchies, each
of which has its own set of inefficiencies. These inefficiencies can
only be rooted out by the people closest to the problems involved.

Think back to the long lines at Denver Licensing. Had Mayor
Hancock tried to improve the city's performance exclusively through
directives from his office, how could he have discovered the inefficiencies that were obvious to Loucks and her staff? The best he could

have done was to throw money at the problem, perhaps engaging outside consultants (who would know far less about the processes than the front-line staff), or maybe by hiring more personnel and adding service windows, while ignoring the underlying causes of the inefficiency.

To get at the operating problems of government, improvement efforts need to be led at the level of the problems they are trying to solve.

Government Is Not a Business

The central premise of Osborne and Gaebler's 1992 book *Reinventing Government*, one of the classics on improving public-sector performance, is that the path to superior public-sector efficiency is for government to be run like a business.[5] The book is well written and persuasive, and it makes a strong case for something that many people have long believed.

But government is not a business. It has a fundamentally different role in our society, operates with a unique set of checks and balances, has a much more complex mission, and answers to a diverse constituency with interests that often conflict. Public-sector managers face an entirely different landscape than their private-sector counterparts. As such, not every business practice translates seamlessly into a government setting. Some need to be modified; others do not work well at all.

In business, if managers want to make changes within their spheres of authority, they can usually do so. If doing so requires resources that they don't already have, generally all they need to do is make the case for the change to their superiors and the resources will be made available. While this is a bit of an oversimplification and is dependent upon the organization, the manager's position, and the specifics of the proposed change, it largely holds true. It is not surprising that CI initiatives where improvement efforts are almost exclusively led by managers and professional staff have proved to be the predominant modus operandi in the private sector.

It seems only common sense that managers and professional staff should lead improvement efforts in the public sector too, and that they should focus on projects that will have the largest impact. But when they do, they typically face significant political, regulatory, and bureaucratic hurdles that can make the process frustratingly slow and inordinately time consuming. It is much more costly—in terms of the time, effort, and emotional energy required—to make medium and large improvements in government than it is in business.

This is not to say that improvements at this level should not be undertaken, because they should. But if a CI initiative is based *primarily* on this type of improvement, it will severely underperform. Not only can fewer improvement projects be completed because of the time and effort involved, but management-driven improvement suffers from the same limitation we just discussed for high-level improvement efforts. As we shall explain in the next chapter, most problems in organizations are buried deeply in their processes and work practices, which makes them invisible to top and middle managers. In other words, management-driven improvement can address only a fraction of the problems an organization faces.

It is normal for top leaders to want to focus on solving big problems, which naturally pushes them toward management-driven improvement and away from front-line–driven improvement. We saw this pattern in many CI initiatives. For example, in one Midwestern state, the head of the CI office told us of his frustration at being swamped with major improvement projects that totally consumed the time of his small staff. He and his people had impressive professional credentials as well as considerable experience in both CI and organizational change. They had come to realize that for their work to have a lasting impact, they needed to embed front-line improvement into the daily operations of the state's agencies. Unfortunately, top administrators relished their newfound ability—through the CI office—to address the problems *they* saw as important, so they kept piling new projects onto the staff.

In another case we studied, the CI office was able to avoid the trap of being consumed by larger projects. In the Colorado Department of Health Care Policy and Financing (think Medicare and Medicaid), the CI office had started out using the Rapid Improvement Event (RIE), the popular CI approach mentioned in the Introduction, that is designed to make quick, often radical, changes to a process. In the private sector, a typical RIE might take one to five days, plus a bit of preparation and follow-up time. However, when the department followed the standard RIE script, it took *eighteen months* to complete the first project. The excessive time was caused by the need to convince many people in different parts of the organization that the changes were needed, to ensure their needs were addressed, to make certain no policies or rules were being violated by the potential solutions, and to get all the departments that might be affected by the changes on board. After the project was completed, the manager in charge of the CI office realized that working on a single large process consumed all of her staff's time and emotional energy. It was a poor use of the small group's improvement capacity. So she streamlined and condensed her RIE process, and then she pared down the size of the problems her group took on. By focusing on more modest issues that could be addressed by getting the right people in a room for an afternoon, her team was able to solve many more problems and significantly increase the pace of improvement. The four-hour RIE became the department's new improvement technique of choice.

Front-Line Improvement—Under the Radar

As we have mentioned, front-line ideas constitute the bulk of the improvement potential in an organization. But in government, they have an important additional advantage. Front-line improvement ideas avoid almost all the obstacles faced by management-driven change. Since most front-line improvements are small, low-cost, and easy to implement, they remain largely invisible, and generally avoid the issue of resistance. And so, provided they have the support of their immediate supervisor, front-line staff can address a host of problems with large numbers of these incremental improvements without higher-level managers or the government bureaucracy ever being aware of the changes.

How, for example, would anyone in city government outside of Denver Licensing become aware of the licensing technician's idea to preassemble the sets of forms needed for specific license applications? Or how would anyone notice that the technicians had created a greatly simplified instruction manual so that applicants would no longer be confused by the software when doing criminal background checks? Even if some of these individual changes were to become known outside of the department, why would anyone complain? They are practical and inexpensive solutions to problems that don't impact anyone outside of the licensing staff and the applicants. And only after many such improvements had eliminated the long lines might city administrators notice that something was different about the licensing department.

The high-performing organization-wide initiatives we studied had a lot of improvement activity going on at all levels, from restructuring major processes to modest front-line adjustments. But there was a distinct difference in how the management-driven improvement projects were run in these organizations. The managers involved integrated a front-line perspective into their problem-solving in a number of ways, such as including front-line staff as members of management-led improvement teams, seeking input on management issues from front-line employees, and getting timely information from front-line staff to inform higher-level decisions. Additionally, synergies were created between larger management-led improvements and front-line improvement activity. Large changes typically need a lot of small adjustments at lower levels to work well, and many issues identified at lower levels need higher-level involvement to fix. By working seamlessly between levels, both management-driven and front-line improvement were made easier and more effective.

While management-led improvement efforts are generally more challenging in government than in the world of business, a case can be made for front-line–driven improvement actually being *easier* in the public sector than in the private sector. During our study, we interviewed hundreds of front-line employees. We were struck by the pride many expressed in working for the government. They believed their work was important and that it was in the service of others and for the greater good. They wanted their units to perform well, and given the opportunity to make improvements, they had no shortage of ideas. In our experience, this strong sense of mission is not so widespread in the private sector.

2

The Power of
Front-Line–Driven Improvement

More than seventy years ago, the Nobel-prize–winning economist Friedrich Hayek provided insight into the unique nature of front-line knowledge. In his essay "The Use of Knowledge in Society," Hayek identified two kinds of knowledge: *aggregate* knowledge, and knowledge *where the particular circumstances of time and place are important*. Upper management generally has aggregate knowledge, gained from high-level data and performance information derived by quantifying, simplifying, and combining the results of the activities taking place across an organization. Such knowledge provides a picture of the organization's overall performance and is necessary for spotting high-level trends, making good strategic decisions, and identifying what aspects of performance need to be improved. But it is largely useless for making specific improvements. For these, the second type of knowledge—knowledge derived from understanding the particular circumstances of time and place—is needed. This knowledge of the day-to-day working of the organization is what front-line workers have. And it puts them in the best positions to spot problems and figure out the best ways to solve them.

To illustrate the richness of Hayek's insight and how it plays out in practice, consider how the Washington State Patrol garage transformed itself from a struggling operation into a national benchmark of efficiency and innovativeness.

Front-Line Ideas at the Washington State Patrol Garage

The Washington State Patrol (WSP) had a problem. An earlier budget crisis had required austerity measures, which had included a freeze on the purchase of new patrol vehicles. This had caused the average mileage of state patrol cars at their retirement from service to rise to over 150,000. When Chief John Batiste talked with patrol officers around the state, the most frequent complaint he heard was that the high-mileage patrol cars were unsafe, unreliable, and frequently out of service for repairs. And the cost of these repairs was eating up an increasing chunk of the WSP's budget.

State funding for new vehicles had eventually been restored, but this did not resolve the problem. The WSP garage had become a bottleneck. It could not convert the newly purchased vehicles into patrol cars fast enough. The conversion process installed radios, lights, light bars, sirens, prisoner partitions, gun locks, flashlight holders, a mobile office (i.e., a computer and cameras), special decals, and many other features.

About twenty people worked at the garage. Half of them were mechanics performing repairs and routine maintenance, and the other half were installers converting vehicles. Over the previous two years, the installers had averaged about twelve conversions per month. Typically, two of these twelve were replacements for patrol cars that had been wrecked in accidents, and ten were replacements for the oldest cars in the WSP's fleet. When the vehicle budget was restored, the garage was suddenly confronted with a large backlog of three hundred new cars awaiting conversion—two and a half years' worth of work. These cars had ended up sitting in the lot for so long that many had moss growing on them. Something had to be done, but the WSP did not have the funds to expand the conversion garage and hire more installers.

Fortunately, an opportunity arose to improve the situation. Governor Gregoire had recently begun an initiative to improve the efficiency of state government. To support this effort, Boeing offered to have several of its corporate trainers conduct a number of one-week lean workshops for state employees.[1] The Deputy Chief in charge of the state's fleet of police vehicles saw this as a potential way to ease the conversion bottleneck, and he asked that one of these workshops be conducted at the WSP garage. As a result, Boeing instructors facilitated a training session attended by about half of the employees from the garage—installers, mechanics, clerks, and supervisors.

Not everyone was excited about the prospect of attending the workshop. The clerk in charge of parts procurement and inventory, for example, complained vehemently that the five-day workshop would be a waste of his time. He was already doing the work of two people because one of the two positions in his area was vacant.

As part of the training, the garage employees created a value stream map of the process for converting factory-fresh vehicles into patrol cars.[2] By the end of the exercise, they had identified fifty-three steps in the process that were redundant, non–value adding, or inefficient. Some steps could easily be eliminated or streamlined, while others would take more time, thought, and resources to change. By the end of the workshop, the initially reluctant parts clerk had become a staunch supporter of the lean improvement process and couldn't wait to start making some of the improvements the group had identified.

Coming out of the workshop, the installers set a goal of increasing the conversion rate from twelve vehicles per month to twenty per month over the next two and a half years—a 67 percent productivity increase. A large whiteboard was put up to manage improvement projects and track results. For the next nine months the installation group met regularly to review progress, discuss problems and ideas, and decide what actions to take next. These meetings eventually grew into weekly improvement meetings of the entire staff, including supervisors.

The first improvements were straightforward procedural changes with immediate impact. For example, a great deal of the installers' time was wasted when they were pulled away from their work to repair previously installed equipment. These repairs should have been done on the maintenance side of the garage, but the mechanics lacked the training to repair some of the specialized electronic equipment. The solution was straightforward. The maintenance and repair supervisor organized training sessions to teach his mechanics how to handle such repairs.

Most problems are buried in an organization's day-to-day processes and work routines. While managers may not notice these issues, front-line employees deal with them all the time.

Another timewaster for the installers was when troopers brought in their cars and requested custom changes to their installed equipment. They might, for example, want flashlight brackets or gun racks switched to different positions. Because the installers wanted to help get the troopers back out on patrol, they would drop whatever they were doing and make the changes on the spot. The installers decided that they would no longer offer such customizing service and would adopt a standardized conversion package for all vehicles. An additional advantage of standardizing the vehicle equipment layout was that officers would not be confused in an emergency if they were using a different patrol car.

One of the larger early projects was to improve the process by which the components and materials needed to make conversions were requested, picked from inventory, and delivered to the installers. The team assembled for the project was led by that initially reluctant parts clerk. All parts, for both the repair/maintenance and the conversion sides of the garage, were stored in a warehouse building next to the main garage, and both sides used the same process for requesting parts. When installers brought in a new car to work on, they would fill out a check sheet requesting the parts they needed and go searching for the parts clerk, who could be anywhere in the warehouse. When the clerk received the check sheet, he would put it in his queue. When its turn came, he would get on his forklift, pick up an empty pallet, and head out to collect the parts. He would pile the parts on the pallet as he went, then drive across to the main building and deliver them to the requesting installer.

This somewhat random process for picking parts meant that they arrived jumbled together on the pallet, and often with some parts missing because they hadn't been checked on the pick sheet or the clerk had missed them. The installers wasted a great deal of time waiting for parts and then searching through the piles for the one they needed next. And when they discovered parts missing, they would have to fill out a new check sheet and wait for the same process to play out again.

The solution comprised several elements. A standard parts list was created for each of the two primary types of vehicle conversion, and a staging area for installation parts was set up in the main garage. The concept was to have the parts for each type of conversion "kitted" and ready to go on special carts that had designated places for each part. After trying several cart options, the group settled on a design and ordered six of them. Now the carts of parts are prepared ahead of time and are ready for the installers to wheel to their work areas when needed.

Many other improvements were made:

- New vehicle keys were being tossed onto a cabinet shelf in a random fashion. Installers would have to hunt through a large pile of keys to find the ones for their next vehicle. Now the keys are attached to the work orders, and no searching is necessary.

■ Vehicles to be converted were parked in a back lot where installers had to search through rows of nearly identical cars for the VIN number of the one that they were assigned to work on next. The parking lot was reorganized so vehicles could be easily found, and those scheduled for conversion next are now lined up just outside the garage.

■ Careful measurement and triangulation were required to get three decals properly positioned and aligned on the doors of patrol cars. Now a magnetic template placed on the door makes proper decal positioning easy. (This idea sparked many additional improvement ideas involving the use of templates to mark where holes should be drilled or items should be mounted.)

■ Instead of the installers cutting and stringing some fifty separate wires to connect all the conversion equipment in the vehicles, wire harnesses—preassembled bundles of wires cut to the right lengths and ending in connection clips—were purchased from a vendor. This saved more than six hours per installation. (Further evolutions of this idea will be discussed later.)

■ Instead of the installers having to drill and tap mounting holes in various brackets, the vendor now delivers the brackets predrilled and pretapped, ready to install.

■ The back seats of police vehicles see a lot of abuse. Previously, the installers replaced the seats with tough, washable plastic seats. The original seats were then stored until the vehicles were decommissioned from service, when they would be reinstalled before the cars were sent to auction. One installer found a supplier that could laser-measure the back seats and computer-cut form-fitting rugged plastic covers for them. This eliminated the need to buy and install plastic seats, cut hours off installation time, saved tens of thousands of dollars in storage costs, and eliminated the labor needed to swap out the plastic seats with the originals when vehicles were decommissioned.

After thirty months the installers were averaging thirty-six conversions per month, *three times* more than before, and well above the goal of twenty they had set for themselves. Conversions were taking much less time, even with a significant increase in the complexity of the new systems and technologies that were now standard equipment—such as more sophisticated mobile offices, upgraded communication equipment, and new video capability. The average fleet vehicle retirement mileage dropped from over 150,000 to less than 110,000 miles, considerably reducing annual maintenance costs.

Once the backlog of vehicle conversions was eliminated, the pace of work settled down to the new normal replacement rate of fifteen to twenty vehicles per month. This gave the installers enough time to start catching up with decommissioning retired patrol vehicles. Before a retired vehicle can be sold as a used car, all police accoutrements must be removed. During the conversion crisis, little attention was paid to decommissioning, and the parking lot had filled with over five hundred retired police vehicles waiting to be processed (over four years' worth), while they were decreasing in value every day.

The installers quickly realized that the decommissioning work could be reduced if they made changes to the *original* conversion process. During decommissioning, for example, many of the holes previously drilled to install equipment or run wires had to be patched. Installers found ways to reduce the size of these holes or eliminate the need for them, making decommissioning easier and the used vehicles more valuable. Interestingly, many of the ideas that made it easier to remove police equipment also made it easier to install in the first place.

The result of all the improvement work was that the decommissioned vehicles sent to auction were newer, higher quality, and lower mileage, putting an additional half a million dollars per year back into state coffers. In fact, with more life left in the retired vehicles, some were now being purchased directly by small local police departments, eliminating the requirement for full decommissioning.

Even things that had previously been improved were fair game for further enhancements. For example, the earlier idea to purchase wire harnesses had saved a lot of installer time, and the standardization it brought made maintenance and repairs easier because mechanics were no longer confronting different wire-stringing patterns depending on who had done the original installation. The problem was that it took a great deal of time and effort to coordinate any changes with the harness supplier, which impaired the installers' ability to make simple wiring modifications. Moreover, the harnesses cost almost $700 each. With time freed up as the decommissioning backlog dwindled away, the idea emerged to bring the assembly of harnesses in-house. Once the installers had mastered the making of harnesses, they were able to come up with a lot of improvements that brought the cost per unit down to under $400 and made the harnesses quicker to install. More importantly, they were much easier to reconfigure. Overall, making the harnesses in the garage saved more than $500 per conversion.

Most front-line work involves repeatedly executing service-delivery processes. As a result, the benefits of even a modest improvement to one of these processes can be surprisingly large.

Since the initial Boeing training, lean has become integral to the way the garage works. New hires are now selected with an eye for their attitudes toward improvement, and they are encouraged to step forward with improvement ideas, especially any better practices/ methods that they may have learned at previous employers. The CI initiative has pushed out beyond the garage as well. Installers work closely with suppliers to identify improvement opportunities that will benefit both parties. The garage has developed a special relationship with Setina, a major supplier of police vehicle equipment. Several ideas from WSP garage installers have led to new Setina products, and many Setina product ideas have been tested and refined at the garage.

The WSP garage has become a national benchmark for the police vehicle conversion process. It regularly hosts visitors who want to understand how to make their own operations more efficient. The lively exchange of ideas during these visits means the learning goes both ways. The garage also sends installers, rather than managers, to trade shows in order to keep up with the latest developments in the industry. This emphasis on front-line learning has come to be central to how the garage is managed.

Key Properties of Small Front-Line Ideas

Although managers played important supporting roles in the transformation at the WSP garage, as they did at Denver Licensing, most of the ideas and initiative came from front-line employees. In the Introduction, we mentioned the 80/20 Principle of Improvement, which states that 80 percent of an organization's improvement potential lies in the creativity and ideas of front-line staff. Even though it has been demonstrated in many different countries and industries, most organizations make little use of this potential.[3] The 80/20 Principle explains why, to be truly effective, CI requires broad-based front-line engagement. In the rest of this chapter, we take a closer look at the reasons behind the extraordinary power in front-line ideas.

REASON 1. *Front-line employees see many problems and opportunities that their managers do not, and they have considerable* *situation-specific knowledge about the work their organization does. As a result, they can come up with plenty of ideas to improve productivity and service levels, to save time and money, or to enhance their organizations in other ways.*

As Hayek pointed out, managers deal primarily with aggregate information. But this kind of information is largely useless for making specific improvements. Most problems and operating inefficiencies are buried in an organization's day-to-day processes and work routines. While managers may not notice these issues, front-line employees deal with them all the time. How would managers at the WSP garage know about the rat's nest of vehicle keys the installers had to dig through? But the installers were certainly aware of the problem—it was a considerable hassle for them.

Front-line employees are also the ones with the detailed knowledge needed to understand the causes of the problems they see, and it is they who can solve these problems in practical and cost-effective ways. Recall the series of ideas about wire harnesses. It is highly unlikely that the shop supervisor would have known as much about the issues involved as the installers who actually strung the wires.

Shigeo Shingo, the codeveloper of lean at Toyota, once wrote, "We must always keep in mind that the greatest waste is the waste we don't see."[4] Most front-line ideas solve problems that are literally *invisible* to management. Without front-line–driven improvement, these inefficiencies simply disappear into the cost of doing business, with management none the wiser.

REASON 2.   *Most front-line improvements in how work is done are deceptively small—their impact is much larger than it seems at first glance. Small changes to processes that are repeated frequently accumulate into a significant advantage.*

Most front-line work involves repeatedly executing service-delivery processes. As a result, the benefits of even a modest improvement to one of these processes can be surprisingly large. Take, for example, the Denver Licensing idea to give each customer service station its own printer, which saved technicians from having to wait in line for the centralized printer. Conservatively, if the idea saved a mere 2 minutes per occurrence, twenty times per day, at each of nineteen stations, the total daily time-savings was 760 minutes, or more than 12 hours per day. This would be equivalent to adding one and a half new technicians! And think of the constant annoyance this change also eliminated for both service technicians and customers.

The WSP garage installers' idea to use wire harnesses, instead of individually stringing fifty separate wires in each vehicle, saved about 6 hours per installation. At twenty conversions per month, twelve months a year, this eliminated a total of 1440 hours, or 180 days of installer time annually.

> Since the problems solved by front-line ideas are buried deeply in the processes of daily work, the benefits of a single improvement remain largely invisible to managers. As such, it is not surprising that the power of front-line ideas is unappreciated by so many managers.

These examples also illustrate another irony of front-line improvements. Since the problems they solve are buried deeply in the processes of daily work, and the benefits of a single improvement pay out as repeated small dividends over time, they remain largely invisible to managers. Their impact

is typically visible only collectively in overall performance statistics that show improvement in cost, productivity, or service
levels, and then only if you are looking for it. As such, it is not
surprising that the power of front-line ideas is unappreciated
by so many managers, who don't see them as playing much of
a role in any organizational improvement effort.

REASON 3.   *Because of the sheer quantity of front-line ideas, they
accumulate to have an enormous overall impact.*

There are a lot of front-line employees, and they have a lot
of ideas. Although most of the organizations we studied did
not keep track of the number of employee ideas they received,
the few that did were averaging about one implemented idea
per person per month. We believe that many of them—one
being the WSP garage—were doing much better than this.
And as explained earlier, most of these ideas will continue to
pay their small daily dividends for years to come. At the WSP
garage, their cumulative impact was dramatic. Over two and a
half years, without adding any new installers, and facing more
complicated conversions, the WSP garage tripled its vehicle
conversion rate.

REASON 4.   *An improvement in one place is often replicable in
many other places, creating a significant multiplier effect.*

Earlier, we briefly mentioned the front-line idea system at
the Colorado Department of Transportation (CDOT) (known as
"Lean Everyday Ideas," it will be fully described in Chapter 8).
A key part of this system is its replication process. Every time
an individual CDOT patrol (think of a highway maintenance
crew with four to six employees) implements an improvement
that might be used by other patrols, it forwards an explanation
of the improvement (usually with photographs) to the Office
of Process Improvement (OPI), located at CDOT headquarters
in Denver. The OPI posts these replicable ideas on its website,

allowing useful ideas from one patrol to be copied by the other 220 patrols around the state.

One idea, for example, reduced the work involved to mount and remove a wing plow (the plow extension on the side of plow trucks) from two hours for two employees, to six minutes for one employee, with greatly improved safety. The improvement involved the fabrication of a specially designed cart, costing less than $200, that held the plow in just the right position for mounting and dismounting. When this idea was uploaded to the website, within months, almost every patrol in the state had built their own cart. In this way, the replication system turned a single idea with local impact into an idea with efficiency and safety implications across the state.

It is important to note that in a large organization like CDOT, improvement ideas do not naturally find their way to everyone that can use them. Some type of formal replication system is needed.

REASON 5.   *Big problems can rarely be solved by management action alone—they also require many small front-line ideas.*

Big problems often have many contributing factors and comprise nests of interconnected subproblems. As such, a collaboration between management and the front lines is needed to address them effectively. Some parts of the problem only management can solve, other parts need a front-line perspective, and still others are best addressed jointly.

The transformation at the WSP garage began because of a big problem—the aging fleet of patrol vehicles. Top management had created the problem, and top management had to contribute toward fixing it by purchasing a large number of additional new vehicles. But that was only the beginning of the story. The rest of the solution depended on the ideas of the front-line installers, who not only solved the original problem, but also dramatically reduced costs and increased the capability of the garage.

REASON 6.   *Front-line–driven improvement creates a learning organization whose capabilities are constantly growing.*

Most front-line improvements are not one-offs. They are copied, modified, built upon, and/or spark entirely new ideas. With each step forward, the organization can be said to "learn," as its improved processes, services, and products allow it to function better. To illustrate this point, let us dig a little deeper into the series of ideas about wire harnesses at the WSP garage.

Before changing to wire harnesses, the installers had to measure, cut, cap, and string more than fifty wires, one at a time, during the conversion process. With each installer using their own technique and wiring patterns, there was a lot of variation in how the vehicles were wired. One of the lessons taught by the Boeing lean instructors was the importance of standardization—a lesson quickly grasped by the installers in this context, as they had all experienced challenges when trying to fix electrical problems in vehicles that had been wired by a colleague. So, one of the issues the installers discussed in their early idea meetings was how to standardize the wiring.

A strong front-line–driven improvement culture allows an organization to take on issues that require creative solutions and an ability to adapt quickly.

This led to the idea of using wire harnesses. Unfortunately, in the beginning, none of the installers had the time or the expertise to make them. By contracting out this work, they could get prefabricated harnesses, with all the wires precut to the correct lengths, fitted with the appropriate connection clips on the ends, and bundled together for easy installation. In addition to saving six hours per conversion, the outsourcing started the installers' education in wire harnesses. They learned how to install them, how to modify them, and eventually, how to make them.

As more and more improvements to the conversion process were made, the outsourcing created a new set of problems. Often, when equipment was added, removed, or relocated, changes were required in the harnesses. And each change triggered a new round of engineering drawings and negotiations with the supplier. The process became so time-consuming and burdensome that the installers began working around it by splicing wire extensions onto the harnesses, or coiling and hiding excess wire. As the installers continued to make changes to the vehicles, the lack of flexibility with outsourced harnesses became increasingly problematic.

As the installers gained experience with the wire harnesses, and the improvements in the conversion process freed up manpower, they realized that they could make the harnesses themselves. And as discussed earlier, bringing the harness assembly in house subjected it to the garage's intense improvement culture. A barrage of improvement ideas quickly dropped the cost well below the outside vendor's price. More importantly, the move created the ability to experiment more easily with new equipment configurations and installation techniques. In the end, the WSP's organizational learning not only saved on the cost of the wire harnesses and reduced their installation time, but created flexibility that further accelerated the pace of improvement.

A similar pattern of learning took place throughout the garage with many aspects of its work. Ultimately, it was this ability to learn rapidly that would transform the garage into a national benchmark.

3

The Critical Role of the
Front-Line Leader

I n the mid-1980s, Fred Luthans, a professor at the University of
Nebraska, led a research project to study how "successful and effective [managers] do things differently from their unsuccessful and
less effective counterparts."[1] His findings were eye-opening, and a
bit unsettling.

Over a four-year period, Luthans's research team tracked and
categorized the activities of 457 different managers in a number of
large companies and government organizations. When the data was
analyzed, the team discovered dramatic differences between "successful" managers—that is, those who were promoted rapidly—and
"effective" managers—those whose units performed well and whose
employees were highly engaged. In common parlance, the terms
successful and *effective* are used interchangeably and would both be
employed to describe *good* managers. But, with Luthans's definitions,
the study found little overlap between the two. Successful managers
were markedly less effective, and effective managers were markedly
less successful.

The differences were explained by how the managers spent their
time. Compared with their effective counterparts, the successful

managers spent roughly four times as much time networking and interfacing with superiors and peers from other units and less than half as much time working with their subordinates. Only a small fraction of the managers, less than 8 percent, ran high-performing units *and* received rapid promotions—that is, they were both effective *and* successful. These managers balanced their time more evenly between networking and working with their subordinates.

At face value, the study supports the cynical view that brown-nosing is the ticket to promotion. The diligent managers who plug away at developing their people and units are naïve and actually *hurting* their chances for promotion.

But we draw a different lesson from Luthans's research, particularly in light of what we observed about the front-line leaders we studied. While Luthans observed a random sample of managers, our sample was highly selective. Because the managers we examined had been singled out to us by their superiors as effective, their bosses clearly already thought highly of them. Arguably, this means the front-line leaders in our study were *both* effective *and* successful. And the perspective we studied them from allowed us to look for potential synergies between their networking behaviors and their unit-building capacities.

> The leaders who were able to collaborate
> with colleagues and superiors to create change
> in their larger organizations were better connected
> and able to secure the institutional support
> needed to help their own units excel.

Where our findings diverged from (or perhaps built upon) those of Luthans was in the impact of some of the behaviors that fall into the category of networking. While the Luthans study linked networking to career success, but found it negatively correlated with effectiveness, we observed that certain kinds of networking had a strong positive relationship to *both* success and effectiveness. The leaders who were able to collaborate with colleagues and superiors to create change in their larger organizations were better connected and able to secure the institutional support needed for their own units to excel. Furthermore, these leaders demonstrated a nuanced understanding of how their decisions and personal behavior affected their subordinates' engagement and professional development.

In the first half of this chapter, we illustrate the power of "institutional street smarts" with an example from the criminal justice system in Minnesota, and then we discuss how front-line leaders can cultivate these street smarts to become significantly more effective at dealing with superiors and their larger organizations. The second half of this chapter deals with a number of counterintuitive practices we observed in our front-line leaders that significantly increased their effectiveness. Many of these practices involved different ways of thinking and responding that were oriented toward the development of subordinates as independent thinkers and problem-solvers. Managing this way required front-line leaders to have a keen sensitivity to how their actions impacted their employees.

Institutional Street Smarts

The front-line leaders in our study were singularly adept at navigating the complex jumbles of rules, policies, and bureaucratic work practices that are commonplace in almost every large government organization. They also demonstrated considerable diplomatic skills in getting things accomplished while dealing with a myriad of personalities and interests. Their institutional street smarts were not only important when working across boundaries in their organizations, but in gaining the confidence of their superiors. This confidence provided the front-line leaders with the leeway to create the local improvement cultures they were after.

A good illustration of how impactful institutional street smarts can be involved Paul Schroeder, a management analyst in the Ramsey County Department of Corrections in Minnesota. Ramsey County is the state's second most populous and includes its capital, St. Paul. Although Schroeder had little formal authority, for over a decade he was the force behind the development of several innovative criminal justice tools that required the cooperation of eighty-seven counties and almost seven hundred police departments and that substantially lowered criminal activity across the state.

In the early 2000s the Ramsey County Department of Corrections had a problem. Whenever people "under supervision" (Minnesota's term for supervised probation or parole) had an encounter with law enforcement personnel—from a warning stop for speeding to an arrest and booking for a felony—they were required to report the incident to their probation officers (POs). But few did. And unless informed by their "clients" (i.e., their supervisees), the POs would rarely find out about the encounters. In addition, a client could be booked for a minor offence, pay a fine, and be released without the local police or judge realizing that the offender was in violation of their terms of supervision and subject to reincarceration or other sanctions. And, although no one knew this at the outset, roughly 40 percent of the people who were booked by police across the state were under some form of supervision. Minnesota had a lot of people on supervision because it made liberal use of supervised release and probation in preference to extended incarceration—a practice which was often credited for the state's low recidivism rates.

Schroeder convinced a computer specialist at the county sheriff's office, Ben Gong, to help him cobble together a system that could notify Ramsey County POs of local bookings of current and previous clients. Gong developed a system that notified POs by email as subjects were booked. The effort caught the attention of Bob Hanson, Assistant Director of Corrections for Adult Probation, whose responsibilities included overseeing the work of the county's POs. He immediately saw the importance of getting this information to the POs in a timely manner.

When talking with his counterpart in Hennepin County (the state's largest, which adjoins Ramsey, and whose county seat is Minneapolis) about the issue of POs not being informed of police encounters, Hanson learned that the Minneapolis Police Department had developed what it called the Police Stop System that captured a great deal of useful information on law enforcement encounters with civilians. The important point for Hanson was that every night when the stop records were uploaded into the county's system, names and birthdates were crosschecked with the database containing people on supervised release in Hennepin Country. If there was a match, the appropriate PO was automatically sent an email with the details of the encounter. The system did everything that Ramsey County's cobbled-together system did, and more. Hanson mentioned this to Schroeder and suggested that he contact Doug Hicks, who oversaw the Minneapolis Police Stop System.

The two met and exchanged information. The primary issue was that no matter how good the Police Stop System was, it reported stops only to Hennepin County POs. The greater Twin Cities metropolitan area covers seven counties and includes the cities of Minneapolis and St. Paul, as well as several dozen suburbs and outlying communities, each of which had its own police department and its own system for recording police stops. If a Ramsey County client was picked up by police in Minneapolis or any of these other communities, their PO would probably never know. Schroeder and Hicks wondered how often this happened, so they decided to run an experiment. Hicks ran the Minneapolis police stop data for the previous month against the Ramsey County database of parolees under supervision. It showed that every day between twelve and twenty Ramsey County parolees had recordable interactions with Minneapolis police. Further investigation by Schroeder found that less than a third of these parolees had reported the incidents to their POs.

It was clearly important for public safety that the POs get full information about police stops of their supervisees so they could take appropriate action. Hicks described the impact of the Minneapolis system as *stealth policing*, because it does not involve the type of crimes and arrests that get reported in the press, but it gets a lot of bad actors off the streets in a very discreet manner. It doesn't solve crimes, but it prevents a lot of them.

With some relatively minor adjustments, and by giving Hennepin County access to the Ramsey County supervision database, every evening when Minneapolis police batch-processed their stop reports, they also ran them against this database and automatically sent emails to the appropriate POs in Ramsey County. The POs loved getting these emails. They were timely and gave the POs a lot of information they did not have before.

With the concept now proven, Schroeder began to think about how to expand it to all eighty-seven counties and seven hundred–plus police departments across the state. He had a good idea of where to start. Among his duties, he was responsible for Ramsey County's Court Services Tracking System (CSTS), the software and database used to manage its criminal justice data. A few years earlier, the approximately thirty counties that used the system had been faced with a crisis. The company that owned the software filed for bankruptcy. At the time, most of the users were at various stages in the process of converting from a DOS-based version of CSTS to a Windows-based version. This had left the counties, of which Ramsey was by far the biggest and most technologically capable, in a bind. The solution to that problem, in which Schroeder played a key role, had been quite creative. The software supplier had previously formed a users' group consisting of representatives from all the counties using CSTS. When the software became tied up in bankruptcy proceedings, this group got together to try to figure out how to acquire the rights to continue using it, finish their conversions, and get ongoing support for the system. Complicating the problem was the fact that under state law, the counties could not act collectively to buy the rights to the software from the bankruptcy without making individual contractual agreements between each pair of counties. Such joint power agreements needed to be signed by the board of each individual county.

Front-line leaders are singularly adept at navigating the complex jumbles of rules, policies, and bureaucratic work practices that are commonplace in almost every large government organization.

Bob Hanson came up with the idea of working through the Minnesota Counties Computer Cooperative (MnCCC). At the time, the MnCCC was a fledgling not-for-profit organization established to support Minnesota counties with various shared software, most of which was for taxation and land management. Hanson's idea was to form a CSTS user group within the MnCCC and to have it purchase the software, provide the necessary ongoing technical support for it, and continue to modify it as new needs and opportunities emerged. The counties that wanted to use the CSTS software could simply join the MnCCC (many were already members) and the CSTS users' group. This structure allowed the counties to work collectively without the need to negotiate individual contracts with every other county and offered budget flexibility when taking on multi-year enhancement projects. The group was also able to get a $1 million grant from the federal Department of Justice, part of which was used to purchase the software and set up the support function. Eventually, eighty-six of the state's eighty-seven counties joined the users' group. (Hennepin County, the lone holdout, joined the group much later.)

Schroeder had played a central role in the CSTS user group. He had helped establish its standards committee, which decided how the system would be adapted and deployed, and had served as its first chairman. He also acted as liaison between Bob Trier, a technical person in the failing company who was willing to help complete the system conversion, and various counties' system administrators. Most of the counties were small compared to Ramsey County and did not have strong technical capability. Schroeder had provided them with significant technical support, earning the gratitude and trust of colleagues across the state. As he explained,

> Collaborative work with people from the other counties is based on trust. Unfortunately, most of these people had had bad experiences working with Ramsey County people from different departments, who tended to throw their weight around. Because Ramsey was the second largest county in Minnesota and had the most resources, its people had often dictated the terms of any collaboration. I was able to rebuild trust by personally helping them with their technical problems.[2]

The contacts that Schroeder had made across the state on the CSTS project were key to implementing his vision of a statewide reporting system for parolee/police encounters. All the necessary information was already in a variety of databases around the state. The challenge was figuring out how to link them. As he put it, "Technically, it was relatively simple. But getting everyone to play was the difficult part."[3] Schroeder's idea was to have each police department upload its stop reports into its CSTS system and then compare this data with all the various parolee records in the other counties' CSTS systems. If a person under supervision was matched to a police stop, a copy of the contact report would be emailed to that person's PO.

Schroeder often collaborated on CSTS issues with an analyst in the Minnesota Department of Corrections, Deb Kerschner. She was coordinating another part of the Department of Justice grant that was to create a state-level database called the Statewide Supervision System (S^3), which would pull together the entire state's incarceration and correction data, including the data on supervised release. Kerschner proposed to Schroeder that the S^3 could be used as a one-stop replacement for having to run the police stop data against the databases of each of the eighty-seven counties individually in search of matches. Schroeder found this change an easy sell to the CSTS users' group.

While POs across Minnesota were grateful for the system because it made their jobs easier and more effective, the law enforcement community took a bit more convincing. Each police department had its own way of recording stops, and many had to modify their systems so the data could be run against the S^3 data. Schroeder gave dozens of presentations to police groups, trying, and for the most part succeeding, to get them to participate. Doug Hicks (his counterpart in Minneapolis, mentioned earlier) developed a simple Microsoft Access application that made the changes easy, even for the smallest police departments. Many officers became converts when they caught on to the stealth policing impact of the S^3 system, and how it would take many bad people off the streets before they committed more serious crimes. Today, the police-stop/CSTS/S^3 comparison process sends out, on average, more than two hundred PO notifications each day statewide.

Had state government leaders ordered a system to be developed, and then mandated the counties to use it, it would have most likely cost several millions of dollars in software and consulting fees, been highly disruptive for the counties, and been much less responsive to local needs. In the end, the S^3 cost Minnesota only $35,000 and a lot of bootlegged time from the many contributors in different counties. It was a model of resourceful unofficial bottom-up development.

Schroeder's ability to understand the various rules and navigate through and around them, while at the same time recruiting the help that he needed and convincing jurisdictions across the state to buy into the idea, is what made the police-stop/CSTS/S^3 comparison process possible. It is worth noting that Schroeder did not always have the enthusiastic support of his superiors. He had to do much of the work on his own time, and he even took vacation days to attend several important meetings. He helped others without any expectation of reciprocity. His power to make improvements derived from his expertise and willingness to help for the greater good.

We came across many examples of front-line leaders using their institutional street smarts to facilitate improvements, both within their units and across their larger organizations. They developed this ability through relationship building and thoughtful observation of how their organizations worked. Some useful advice in this regard emerged from our interviews with Schroeder and other front-line leaders:

- Be helpful to others whenever you can be. This builds trust and engages the principle of reciprocity.

- Focus on the greater good. When you do, as one front-line leader put it, "People are generally willing to help you because they want to be on the side of the angels."

- Take an active interest in your larger organization and learn how it works. When you don't understand how something works, ask others, including high-level managers inside or outside of your chain of command. But while doing this, be careful to keep your own boss appropriately informed.

- Build solid working relationships with managers both upstream and downstream from your group, as well as with key people in support functions. While ensuring that your unit gets the support it needs, make it as easy as possible for them to deal with your unit.

- Manage your relationship with your boss. One front-line leader whose bosses changed frequently became adept at learning how each new boss liked to operate—the frequency, form, and type of communications they preferred; their leadership styles; when they expected independent action and when they wanted to be more involved; and the best way to pitch new ideas to them.

After observing and interacting with a lot of front-line managers, it was clear to us that almost any manager can develop, or at least significantly enhance their institutional street smarts, but it takes thoughtful effort and situational awareness.

The Savvy Front-Line Leader

In addition to street smarts, the front-line leaders we studied had developed an unusually nuanced understanding of how their behavior and problem-solving approach affected their subordinates. Their more sophisticated behaviors and thinking showed in a number of dimensions, including 1) a deliberate patience when setting up and running their improvement efforts; 2) the nature of their interactions with their employees; and 3) the ability to manage their staff through intrinsic motivation.

Going Slow to Go Fast

The front-line leaders in our study practiced an *active patience* when it came to improvement. Instead of pushing for quick results, they took the time to instill the right mindsets in their employees. They created local improvement infrastructures, trained their people, and helped them acclimate to a very different environment in which they were expected to continually improve their work. While this groundwork was being laid, little progress was made on improving performance. But once all the components were in place, improvement was rapid. For the first nine months of Stacie Louck's tenure at Denver Licensing, wait times held steady. But over the next nine months, they were cut by 93 percent, despite an increase in the number of licenses being issued. It was a classic case of going slow to go fast.

The gearing-up phase of a unit's CI initiative can be challenging, particularly in finding ways to free up the necessary staff time for training and for working on early improvement ideas. There is no getting around the fact that if employees are going to spend time making improvements, they will have less time for their regular work. When the WSP installers spent a week in training, for example, they were not working on conversions, and the garage fell even further behind.

Never be too busy to find out how to be less busy.

Another way in which savvy front-line leaders went slow to go fast was in how they handled individual improvement ideas. Before implementing anything but the most straightforward improvement, they invested time and effort to get input from all affected parties. This not only resulted in better and more readily implementable ideas, but it greatly reduced potential resistance to the change. A little extra time spent up front makes the entire improvement cycle—from the discovery of the problem through to the implementation of the solution—much smoother and faster.

For example, the employee idea to improve the department's filing efficiency by digitizing the licensing records at Denver Licensing was obviously a winner. However, had Stacie Loucks immediately jumped on it and started assigning employees to digitize documents, the conversion would not have had nearly the impact it did. But by using the conversion as an opportunity to purge old files, by checking with the other city departments that also used license records (police, fire, health and safety, revenue, etc.) to understand their needs, and by consulting with the IT group on how best to integrate digitized records into the city's existing intranet platforms, she was able to leverage the change to deliver a much broader set of benefits. Now any city employee who needs access to a licensing record can get it instantly online.

"Never be too busy to find out how to be less busy." We came across this wise piece of advice in an old Air Force training program while studying the massive industrial improvement effort made in the US during World War II. One of the more dramatic applications of this concept was in the shipbuilding industry. After the Fall of France in June 1940, the US government realized that it would need to dramatically ramp up production of critical war supplies. Some industries had to increase output by more than 1,000 percent within a year, which would have been impossible without significantly improved processes. The entire US industrial base needed a huge dose of continuous improvement. This was provided by the federal War Manpower Commission's Training Within Industry (TWI) programs. These were a series of training programs set up by the commission when it realized that a big bottleneck to increased production would be a shortage of trained workers and qualified supervisors in the nation's factories. Many skilled workers and their supervisors would be drafted, and their places would be filled with inexperienced people who had never worked in such environments before. By the end of the war, the TWI programs had taught millions of newly minted supervisors how to lead using a precursor of today's front-line–driven improvement. A key message was that time invested in making improvements pays a very high return. For example, at the start of the war it took an average of 1.4 million labor hours and 355 days for Kaiser Shipbuilding (a big TWI user) to build a Liberty ship. Less than two years later, the company had dropped this to 500,000 labor hours and 41 days per ship. Eventually, the ships became so inexpensive that their payback period was literally their *first* completed trip across the Atlantic! At a time when every labor hour was critical, this icon of wartime production power diverted significant resources from building ships to improving *how* ships were built.

Using Everyday Interactions with Subordinates to Develop Them as Improvers

Another subtle set of behaviors that we noticed in our front-line leaders was in their routine interactions with their staff. Front-line supervisors are continually bombarded by subordinates with questions and problems. The natural tendency, and the quickest and easiest thing to do, is to answer the questions and give solutions to the problems. In some situations, this may also be the right thing to do. It certainly moves the work forward expeditiously. However, when this reaction is the default in *all* situations—when the leader answers *every* question and personally addresses *every* problem—employees become dependent upon the boss to do all the thinking. It undermines the mission of creating the engaged, proactive, and capable workforce needed for front-line–driven improvement.

There are times, of course, when managers do need to make decisions and solve problems. But often, and when appropriate, we observed the front-line leaders using queries as teaching moments. Rather than simply answering the question, they might ask for the employee's perspective and discuss it with them. And rather than offering the solution to a problem, the leader might encourage the employee to solve it. Whenever possible, the object was to get employees to think for themselves.

How these front-line leaders responded to a specific question depended upon both the nature of the situation and the employee(s) involved. Was this the right time to be a teacher, coach, or mentor? Did the employee have the knowledge, information, and authority needed to take independent action? If not, what did they need, and was this the time to provide it?

This filtering of interactions with staff was so smooth that at first it seemed to be a natural part of these leaders' personalities. However, when we discussed it with them, we were struck by how often it was the result of a deliberately cultivated and practiced skill. The front-line leaders put considerable effort into getting to know each of their employees, what they valued, how to motivate them, and the knowledge and skills they needed to develop.

Leading with Intrinsic Rather Than Extrinsic Motivation

Another marked aspect of the front-line leaders' savvy was how they worked primarily with *intrinsic*, rather than *extrinsic*, motivation. We found their emphasis on intrinsic motivation interesting and unusual, as the use of extrinsic rewards has become almost ubiquitous. From praise and punishments as children, through grades and gold stars during our education, to the promotions, merit raises, bonuses, and other incentives used in the workplace, extrinsic rewards are widely assumed to be the best way to elicit desired behaviors. While rewards and threats can gain rapid compliance and motivate a person doing rote or algorithmic work, a great deal of research has documented that extrinsic motivation undermines commitment, curiosity, and creativity—all three of which are required for front-line–driven improvement.[4]

So why do experienced leaders, who should know better, still cling to extrinsic rewards? For one thing, they are obvious and easy to use. But researchers have also discovered that people have an "Extrinsic Motivation Bias."[5] While people generally see *themselves* as being motivated primarily by intrinsic factors, they tend to believe that *others* are motivated primarily by extrinsic factors.

> While people generally see themselves as being motivated primarily by intrinsic factors, they tend to believe that others are motivated primarily by extrinsic factors.

Complicating the picture further, extrinsic motivation is often thought of in terms of dangling overt rewards in front of employees. But its use is actually much more pervasive than this. It is subtly embedded in the myriad of small daily interactions between supervisors and their employees. Every time managers use their authority to get a subordinate to do something, they are (perhaps without realizing it) using extrinsic motivation. Authority comes with a significant package of implicit sanctions and favors that are woven into the fabric of the supervisor-subordinate relationship. It is easy to exercise this authority without conscious awareness of its impact on an employee's attitude and behavior. It simply flows naturally from being the boss.

Leading with intrinsic motivation requires patience, self-awareness, and vigilance. In our interactions with employees in the front-line–driven units, we were struck by their strong sense of mission. They were proud of their work and of being part of something bigger than themselves. And their strong intrinsic motivation was no accident—it was consciously built and reinforced by their supervisors.

In his book *Drive,* Daniel Pink laid out a simple framework of the factors involved in promoting intrinsic motivation.[6] Its elements are

- Purpose: Be in the service of some greater good.

- Mastery: Possess the skills and knowledge needed to perform the desired tasks well.

- Autonomy: Have the ability to make decisions and act independently.

The front-line leaders in our study paid careful attention to these factors. They created purpose through their higher-order visions, promoted mastery with training and coaching in CI, and then gave their people the autonomy to solve the problems they were facing.

4

Creating and Developing a Local Improvement Culture

Shortly after Ted Burley was appointed director of the Business Services branch in the Corporate Service department of the Regional Municipality of York in Ontario, Canada, he conducted a review of his branch's service delivery in order to better understand its work and the needs of its customers. His staff of twenty-two provided a range of services to the other six branches in the department, including support for budgeting and finance, communications, and process improvement. Burley had previously headed the region's CI office, and was anxious to instill a strong improvement ethos in his new branch.

He began by setting up structured interviews with the management teams of the other six branches. Depending upon the size of the branch, these meetings involved between four and fourteen managers. Burley started the meetings by asking each participant to relate one good experience, and one bad experience, they had when working with Business Services. Then he worked with the managers to distill this information into two improvement recommendations for his branch. After the six meetings, Burley had a list of twelve recommendations: eight specific requests, and four more broad-based suggestions about how Business Services could interact better with the other six branches.

Burley convened a meeting of his management team to discuss the recommendations. The team quickly decided that all twelve had merit and follow-through on the eight specific requests was assigned to the appropriate managers. Some examples of these requests were

■ Convert the manual job evaluation process to an online form that would make it easier to collect information, compare different jobs, and update job descriptions when the work changed.

■ Automate the Staff Transfer Request Form to save HR considerable time and effort, eliminate manual intervention and errors, and reduce union grievances.

■ Create a "Coffee Chat" program that would allow staff to meet virtually with members of the department that they would not otherwise have reason to connect with. The goal would be to break down silos and bring people together to discuss problems that impacted the entire department.

■ Provide more complete financial information to make it possible to better understand where a branch stood financially.

The request for more complete financial information turned into an extensive project with several improvement iterations. The result was a real-time financial dashboard that allowed each branch to access its complete financial data easily, track transactions in real time, and perform different types of analysis including checking performance against the budget and comparing variances between periods.

The four less-specific recommendations required some serious rethinking about various aspects of how the branch functioned, particularly how its staff worked with clients. These included suggestions such as "Create a closer partnership with us," "Include us in meetings that impact our branch," and "Listen to our perspectives when making decisions that affect us."

Not long after the meeting with his management team, Burley held an all-hands workshop for his branch. He explained the process he had gone through and described the eight specific requests that the management team had already started implementing. He then presented the four general recommendations and asked for the staff's help in figuring out the best ways to address them. After some discussion, the staff divided into four groups, each of which was assigned one of the recommendations to work through using York's "ILab" group problem-solving process (described in more detail in Chapter 12). The resulting action items were later refined by the management team and became the foundation of the branch's improvement agenda for the coming year. Once this agenda was set, Burley presented it to the management teams of the other six branches and enlisted their support.

Burley's review process served several purposes. It familiarized him with his branch's work and gave him an opportunity to start developing relationships with his primary clients. As for his staff, it both emphasized the importance that Burley put on listening to clients and identified some clear improvement areas. But perhaps most importantly, Burley sent a clear message to his people about how he wanted to lead—and that was with their active involvement in making the branch better.

To create a front-line–driven culture in a smooth and robust manner requires an understanding of key leverage points, why they are important, and how to use them effectively.

In making these changes in his branch, Burley had some advantages that most front-line leaders do not have. First, because his prior job was heading the York Region's CI office, he had extensive experience with improvement tools and techniques. Second, he had experience leading service reviews in previous roles at York. Lastly, Burley was confident that he had the support of his superiors. The top leadership of the five-thousand-person York Region government was working diligently to develop a culture of improvement throughout the entire organization.

Most front-line leaders do not start out with the levels of technical knowledge, experience, and support that Burley had. They often begin with little more than a desire to improve their units and the notion that their employees need to be part of the process. For them to create a front-line–driven culture in a smooth and robust manner, they need to understand key leverage points and how to effectively use them, as Burley did. This is what we turn to next.

A Practical Schema for Selling the Improvement Agenda

In the late 1960s and early 1970s, University of Pennsylvania psychologist Martin Seligman discovered something unexpected while conducting a series of experiments on conditioning. When the dogs in his study were repeatedly given electric shocks that they could not escape from, after a while, they just laid down and accepted the pain. Later, when the dogs were given a clear path to escape, they made no effort to do so, and continued to passively accept the shocks. Seligman called this phenomenon *learned helplessness*. Since that time, learned helplessness has been studied extensively in humans (without the shocks, of course) and has become a staple of behavioral psychology.

The concept explains why many front-line employees can come to work every day and passively accept existing conditions such as the long lines at Denver Licensing or the huge backlog of conversions at the WSP garage. It applies in two ways. First, after years of working in top-down environments—where they expect to be told what to do and how to do it—employees have learned from experience that they are expected not to question how their work is done. Offering suggestions is often construed as complaining or challenging authority. Second, employees have lived with the organization's problems for so long that they simply accept these problems as something they have to live with. Many of the front-line leaders in our study were faced with the challenge of overcoming their staff's deeply-conditioned reluctance to get involved in improvement activity. It takes a well-executed change strategy to transform a culture of accepting the status quo into one with an ethos of relentless and ongoing improvement.

When Dean Schroeder was a doctoral student at the Carlson School of Management at the University of Minnesota, he attended a talk given by a visitor, Jay Galbraith, a well-known expert in the field of organizational development. At one point, Galbraith made an observation that stuck with Dean, and which we both now use regularly in our own work. It was a simple schema of three things that people need in order to change:

1. An understanding that change is needed

2. A vision of what they will be changing to

3. A means to get from here to there

If a leader's change strategy lacks any of these elements, their people are more likely to be skeptical about the proposed change and cling to the status quo.

While the three elements are nominally ordinal—for example, you need to know change is needed before developing a new vision, and you need to know where you are going before figuring out how to get there—the transitional actions taken by front-line leaders in our study often engaged all three elements at the same time.

How Front-Line Leaders Get Their Staff Engaged

The noted policy analyst Aaron Wildavsky once observed that "A difficulty is a problem only if something can be done about it."[1] Unless people can see a way to solve a problem, it is just a difficulty they must live with. In a nutshell, the front-line leaders we observed turned difficulties into problems that their people could solve—admittedly not with a single big idea, but with a constant stream of smaller ones. By defining the difficulty, breaking it down into measurable components, providing their people with the ability to address these components through CI training, and then giving them *permission* and *encouragement* to come up with improvement ideas, the leaders were working on all three of Galbraith's elements. And once the overarching problem was solved, the leader moved them on to other improvement opportunities.

Creating a Local Improvement Vision

A good local vision inspires people to pull together to achieve a shared goal.[2] While the overarching purpose of a vision in our context might be to transform a unit into one that is capable of continuously improving and providing outstanding service, the front-line leaders in our study invariably started with local improvement visions built around tangible goals that everyone could agree upon and contribute to achieving. Stacie Loucks used the vision of eliminating wait times as an issue that everyone could rally around. But to bring this vision to life, she made it actionable by having Melissa Wiley gather data to document the extent of the problem, ferret out the factors contributing to it, and set up some simple tracking metrics. These metrics kept the issue front and center for her staff, and as improvements were made along the way, everyone could see how their ideas were chipping away at what had seemed an insurmountable problem.

People need three things in order to change: 1) An understanding that change is needed, 2) A vision of what they will be changing to, and 3) A means to get from here to there.

Ted Burley did not have the advantage of an obvious performance gap to build his unit's improvement vision around. He needed to design a process to discover his branch's major improvement opportunities.

Many managers make the mistake of simply declaring an improvement vision, whether it is their own or one based on a goal passed down from above, and then trying to "sell" it to their subordinates. However, as we discussed in the last chapter, front-line–driven improvement depends on intrinsic motivation. A vision will not inspire many front-line ideas unless it articulates something that is important to employees. A good way to ensure that a vision does this is to involve employees in *creating* it. Recall that the ambitious goal of the WSP garage was set by the installers themselves—and they ended up exceeding it by almost a factor of two. Tangible goals, backed by well-conceived metrics, concentrate ideas on what is important and legitimize ideas that might otherwise be ignored. It is hard to shoot down a reasonable idea that improves a key metric.

Building People into Capable Improvers

A considerable body of knowledge about CI has been built up in the last 150 years, and there is a wide variety of methodologies and training programs to choose from. Each has its own vocabulary and set of techniques. While a number of different methodologies were used by the front-line–driven improvement initiatives we studied, the initiatives all had three basic attributes in common. First, the front-line leaders in our study all made sure that their people received at least a short training course on the basics of continuous improvement. Second, this course emphasized *process improvement, problem identification,* and *problem-solving.* And third, the training required employees to use what they learned to make improvements in their own workplaces.

Process thinking is fundamental to becoming an effective improver. Without process awareness, it is easy for staff to focus narrowly on their individual operations and make "improvements" that either create problems for coworkers in downstream operations or have no real impact on overall process performance. Improvements need to be conceived with an understanding of their impact on the whole process, not just a single component of it. (More on process improvement in Chapter 9.)

The two other topics that the training program emphasized—problem identification and problem solving—usually involved how to define and spot waste, the use of root-cause analysis to solve problems at their source rather than merely addressing symptoms, and the importance of data to understand a problem and permanently eliminate it.

A final common attribute we noticed in the training was that participants were required to make improvements in their work areas either as part of the classroom training itself, or immediately afterward. (Recall, for example, that during the Boeing training, WSP garage installers analyzed their own processes, and came up with fifty-three improvement opportunities.) This training was often followed up with coaching and support that helped the employees apply their new skills to increasingly challenging problems. Direct supervisors typically received more extensive CI training so they could provide much of this coaching to their employees.

Without process awareness it is easy for staff to focus narrowly on their individual operations and make "improvements" that either create problems for coworkers in downstream operations or have no real impact on overall process performance.

Although the initial training was relatively short, it was often only the first step in the ongoing development of CI skills. The organization in our study with the most extensive training regime was the UK's Royal Mint, whose improvement systems we describe in some detail in Chapter 11. The Mint has been forced to have a strong improvement culture for centuries in order to stay ahead of increasingly sophisticated counterfeiters. To keep its employees' technical and CI skills sharp, the Mint makes extensive use of training matrices to monitor the currency of the skills every employee needs for their particular position. On a set schedule, which for some skills can be annually, the checkmarks on the training matrix are erased, and workers have to requalify on those skills.

Making Improvement Part of Everyone's Job

As discussed earlier, many employees are conditioned by experience to believe that improvement is management's responsibility. To change this view requires more from leaders than encouraging rhetoric and good intentions. It means modifying work practices and systems to create the expectation that improvement is *everyone's* job.

Stacie Loucks made it clear in many ways that she needed her employees to engage with the improvement process. She worked to create a shared vision, got everyone trained, and provided all the resources, coaching, and support that employees needed to implement their ideas. She also instilled accountability by including improvement ideas as a factor in the annual review process.

Her staff could also see that Loucks was taking the lead on some of the bigger improvements herself. She convinced the budget committee to reallocate the inspector positions, changed the phone-answering protocols and recruited the 311 unit to help improve responsiveness to customer phone calls, and secured Melissa Wiley's help from Peak Academy. She willingly invested money in good ideas from her staff, such as the one to buy printers for each workstation to eliminate the central printer bottleneck. In short, her staff could see that the rules had changed, and Loucks expected them to play a primary role in improving performance.

A similar pattern played out with the other front-line leaders we studied. They created strategies to eradicate learned helplessness and to get employees actively looking for and solving problems.

Supporting Subordinates without Removing Their Ownership of Problems

The front-line leaders we observed took a very measured approach when employee ideas required their personal involvement. They were judicious in their interventions and always tried to keep as much decision-making with their subordinates as possible. Consider how commanders in the central Stockholm police force helped their patrol officers when the latter asked for help with a frustrating and recurring problem.

Often, the patrol officers would detain a suspect for a crime and bring that person to the station for processing, only to encounter him back on the streets a few hours later. Clearly, something was wrong.

The normal booking procedure was for officers to bring perpetrators into the station, put them in a holding room, fill out the necessary paperwork, and then go back out on patrol. When a member of the prosecutor's office was available, they would come down to the holding area, go through the paperwork, interview the perpetrator, and determine if charges should be filed and whether the suspect should be remanded into custody.

The problem was that the prosecutor would frequently choose not to press charges when the police officers thought they had a solid case. The officers posted this problem on their idea board, but they could do little about it themselves. They had no influence over how the prosecutors worked.

A watch commander saw the problem on the board, approached the chief prosecutor, and together they assembled a team of officers and prosecutors to address it. The team identified the primary cause of the inappropriate releases as the prosecutors' lack of information due to poor communication between them and the arresting officers. When down in the holding area, the prosecutors typically had to make their decisions based solely on arrest reports and their interviews with the suspects because the arresting officers would already be back out on patrol. And after hearing only the suspect's side of the story, the prosecutors often determined that they did not have a strong enough case to proceed, so they released the suspect.

The team realized that the officers frequently had critical information that went beyond what they could easily put in an arrest report and proposed a change to the booking process. Whenever possible, a prosecutor should talk directly with the arresting officers when a suspect was booked. If a prosecutor was not available, or if additional information was required, the arrest report should include the arresting officers' cellphone numbers so the prosecutors could contact them while the officers were out on patrol.

The new procedures resulted in much closer working relationships between the officers and the prosecutors as well as much better decisions in terms of both initial arrests and prosecutions. The officers learned more about the evidence that was needed for effective prosecutions, and the prosecutors learned more about the realities the officers faced.

Note how the problem was solved by the patrol officers and first-level prosecutors, but the opportunity to solve it came about only because of the direct involvement and support of their superiors. The watch commander had to convince the chief prosecutor's office that there was a problem, and supervisors on both sides had to agree to set up the problem-solving team and provide its members with release time. And once the team proposed its solution, these front-line leaders had to get the suggested new procedure approved at higher levels and then implemented. This involved documenting the new procedures, making operational adjustments, and communicating the changes to the staff.

But most importantly, the watch commander and chief prosecutor did *only* what they needed to. They were careful not to take ownership of the problem away from their front-line people. It is not always easy to strike the right balance between jumping in and standing back. But to create and reinforce a front-line–driven environment, supervisors must navigate each improvement situationally, keeping the thinking and acting with the employees as much as possible.

PART 2

Creating Organization-Wide Front-Line–Driven Improvement

In Part 1, we took the perspective of the front-line leader, whose goal is to drive improvement in a small department or group. Part 2 focuses on how to create a front-line–driven culture across large departments and agencies, or entire cities and states. Here, top leaders must work indirectly, implementing their vision through entrenched bureaucracies and multiple layers of managers. In this part, we describe how the top leaders in our study systematically created operating environments that drove front-line improvement throughout their organizations.

We begin with the story of the Canadian Province of New Brunswick, where a severe financial crisis prompted its leaders to create a world-class CI ecosystem across all its departments. With the New Brunswick example as a backdrop, Chapter 6 looks at what it takes to lead such a large-scale organizational transformation, and Chapter 7 explains the infrastructure needed to drive the initiative all the way down to the front-line level.

5

What Transforming a Large Organization Involves: The Case of New Brunswick

Note: This chapter draws in part from an article we wrote for the *Journal of Government Financial Management*. We are grateful to the journal for permission to incorporate that material here.[1]

In 2011, the Canadian Province of New Brunswick faced a severe budget crisis. To address it, the provincial government cut the budget of every department (i.e., ministry) by 7.5 percent. Most deputy ministers (the civil-service department heads) were able to cover much of the shortfall with the usual "cut-and-control" tactics: reducing travel and training, freezing hiring, restricting overtime, deferring maintenance and capital expenditures, and taking other short-term actions to bridge the gap. But when 2012 brought another 7.5 percent budget cut, a different approach was needed if severe reductions in mandated services were to be avoided.

New Brunswick's financial challenges were structural—they were not going to go away without fundamental changes. Located on the Atlantic coast, New Brunswick is one of the four original provinces that formed the Dominion of Canada in 1867. Its population of just over 750,000 was aging, and its economy—with leading sectors in forest products, mining, and services—had been largely stagnant for several years. The government had to find a way to reduce the cost of its operations across the board. Fortunately, the Minister of Finance, Blaine Higgs, had anticipated the problem and had a model in mind for how to do so.

As Minister of Finance, one of the units within Higgs's responsibility was Alcool NB Liquor (ANBL), the government-owned corporation responsible for alcohol distribution and sales throughout the province. Recently, he had been briefed on its results and had been very impressed. Over the previous several years, ANBL had shown strong improvement in net income, customer satisfaction, and employee engagement. In 2011, it was named one of the best one hundred places to work in Canada. Much of this improvement resulted from the CI program championed by Jane Washburn, one of ANBL's vice presidents. Drawing on her private sector experience, Washburn had implemented a CI program combining Lean Six Sigma with a Balanced Scorecard approach.[2] During the briefing on ANBL's results, Higgs had asked Washburn if the same approach could be used across the provincial government as a whole, with its more than 45,000 employees. After some thought, she responded that it would be challenging, but she was keen to experiment with CI practices in the government.

Over the next few months, at the minister's request, Washburn presented the approach used at ANBL and its results to a number of different groups of government leaders. Quite quickly, the deputy ministers, who were desperate for better ways to deal with the cutbacks, became open to a similar approach being adopted provincewide.

As a result, Washburn was asked by New Brunswick's leadership to spearhead an effort to integrate CI into the daily operations of the provincial government. She put together a small staff and began developing the required infrastructure, processes, and employee training and development programs. Ultimately this led to the creation of the Office of Strategy Management (OSM) with Washburn as its chief, reporting directly to the Clerk of the Executive Council, New Brunswick's top civil servant administrator. Washburn and her group developed what became known as the *Formal Management System (FMS)*. The FMS is an overarching management system that incorporates three key components:

1. It clarifies and quantifies the government's high-level strategic goals.

2. It translates these goals into actionable items and deploys them across all the province's departments using a Balanced Scorecard approach.

3. It includes five CI approaches designed to cover the full spectrum of problems that staff will encounter as they work toward these goals.

New Brunswick's CI initiative launched in April 2012. When Washburn announced that she was looking for departments to volunteer for the pilot phase, she had more volunteers than she could handle, despite the significant requirements for participants. First, each deputy minister had to commit to resourcing several new positions—an Alignment Champion and at least one Process Improvement Facilitator. Larger departments, and those with a stronger commitment to CI, often employed more than one facilitator. The Alignment Champion had to be a member of the department's leadership team. They would be responsible for ensuring the department's programs, metrics, and improvement efforts were aligned with the province's primary goals. The Process Improvement Facilitators would be trained as Lean Six Sigma black belts over a fourteen-week period, and then they would act as coaches to initiate, support, and oversee their department's improvement activities. In addition, the entire leadership team of each volunteering department, including the deputy minister, would be required to attend five days of FMS leadership training.

Two key decisions that set up New Brunswick's initiative for success were 1) to integrate CI into the FMS, and 2) to create the OSM, which would report directly to the Clerk of the Executive Council. Using the FMS as the central vehicle for New Brunswick's leaders to deploy and monitor progress toward their key strategic goals, the OSM was able to embed CI into the Balanced Scorecard approach. Cascading the Balanced Scorecard metrics down the hierarchy made managers at all levels accountable for their unit's improvement performance, and the CI tools and techniques included in the third component of the FMS provided them with the means to deliver this improvement. Even the deputy ministers were held accountable. As part of the FMS, deputy ministers have quarterly meetings with the Clerk of the Executive Council, where the overall performance of their departments on strategic priorities, including CI, is reviewed.

> The measured rollout allowed the province
> to learn from each wave and adjust before
> the next. It also allowed the Office of Strategy
> Management to concentrate its limited
> resources in order to ensure success.

Washburn launched the CI effort with a roll-out strategy involving three waves. The first, or pilot wave, of six departments occurred in fiscal 2012–2013. The second, of seven additional departments, came in fiscal 2013–2014; and the final wave in fiscal 2014–2015 included the last ten departments. The launch focused on the Lean Six Sigma and Balanced Scorecard component of the FMS. Once these basic elements were in place, additional CI approaches were added over time to broaden the spectrum of problems that could be addressed and to promote increasing involvement in CI across the government, particularly on the front lines.

The measured rollout allowed the province to learn from each wave and adjust before the next. It also allowed the OSM to concentrate its limited resources in order to ensure success, which created momentum that broadened support for the effort.

Starting with Lean Six Sigma, five distinct but integrated CI approaches were phased in over a few years. This gave people time to learn and use each approach before being asked to learn the next one. In hierarchical order, from the highest-level problem-solving technique on down, the five approaches are value-stream mapping, Lean Six Sigma, Rapid Improvement Events, Waste Walks, and Daily Management.

> **Value-stream mapping** is an approach to better understand a process and identify where to focus improvement efforts. The first time it was deployed by the province was in an attempt to fix a complex scheduling problem in the Moncton Provincial Court. This was the highest-volume court in New Brunswick and had the longest delays.
>
> One of the New Brunswick Department of Justice's black belts led a team of court employees in the improvement initiative. They began by creating a value-stream map designed to highlight delays in the judicial process. An analysis of this map showed that the main cause of the scheduling problem was the high number of adjournments. Most defendants appeared in court multiple times before they could even enter a plea—some as many as fifteen times. The multiple adjournments occurred for many reasons, including defendants lacking legal representation, prosecutors needing more time to provide complete discovery of evidence, and missing paperwork. The sheer number of adjournments was creating havoc with scheduling.
>
> The team developed a number of improvements to lessen the delays:
>
> - ■ To make certain that defendants and their lawyers have the right information up front, an Early Resolution

Package is distributed to each defendant before their first court appearance. It clearly outlines the charges, the Crown's sentencing position on an early guilty plea, and a copy of the person's criminal record for defense counsel.

■ Seventy-five percent of trials were postponed on the first day because the participants were not ready. To ensure that both sides were prepared, and to encourage the resolution of as many issues as possible before the trial started, mandatory pretrial meetings of the opposing counsels were instituted for all trials scheduled to last a full day or longer.

■ Previously, each judge had managed their own schedule. On any given day, one judge might have four quick adjournments and spend the day in chambers, while another judge had to send people home because they had too many cases. The team proposed that the court operate with a master scheduling system in which a court administrator would assign judges to cases on the day of appearance, in order to optimize judicial resources.

These and many other smaller system fixes created a justice process that was much more efficient and had fewer delays. For several tasks, the time of CAD$300,000-per-year judges was replaced by that of CAD$40,000-per-year administrative assistants. Additional savings were realized in witness fees, jury fees, prisoner transportation costs, and translation costs (in New Brunswick, the accused have the right to be tried in either French or English).

More on value-stream mapping in Chapter 10.

Lean Six Sigma projects attack improvement opportunities that require careful problem definition, significant data-gathering and analysis, and often considerable time in order to solve. One project at the Vehicle Management Agency (VMA) addressed problems with spare parts used to maintain the agency's more than 4,300 snowplows, school buses, and light fleet vehicles. The VMA had a network of thirty-one repair facilities, each with a stockroom to source and supply parts for the maintenance operations, and forty-nine smaller satellite operations divisions that also obtained parts through these stockrooms. On an annual basis, the system made 190,000 transactions dealing with 34,000 different kinds of parts and purchased some CAD$15 million of inventory, keeping an average of CAD$5 million in parts on hand. The problem was that the parts management system was cumbersome and inefficient, and kept vehicles off the road for long periods while they waited for parts.

While the OSM provides centralized leadership and clear focus to New Brunswick's CI effort, at the same time, individual departments maintain responsibility for the actual improvement efforts, enabling them to take on the improvement opportunities most appropriate for their goals.

To deal with the problem, the VMA put together a cross-functional team of stockroom staff, accounts-payable staff, and shop-floor mechanics and supervisors. A Lean Six Sigma black belt from the province's Department of Transportation was assigned to facilitate the project. The team spent months gathering and analyzing data, identifying problem areas, and coming up with improvements. For example:

- Previously, every time a mechanic went to the stockroom, the process required the staff to print out a requisition form and have the mechanic sign it. This created a lot of paperwork that would later have to be reconciled and filed. The team designed a new process that required only one requisition form per mechanic per day on which all items used would be recorded.

- A study of how stockroom staff were spending their time showed they were spending a lot of it on the cumbersome paperwork for parts transactions. The team was able to streamline processes and paperwork and to eliminate some thirty-five thousand transactions per year.

- The team calculated that the overall parts inventory was turning over about two times per year. This meant, loosely speaking, that the average part stayed on the shelves for six months. Since 95 percent of parts could be obtained from local suppliers within a few days, inventory could be drastically cut *with no impact* on shop-floor operations. After further analysis, a system-wide 5S effort freed up space. (*5S* is a set of procedures designed to keep only what is necessary and have a place for everything and everything in its place.) The freed-up space allowed the stockrooms to inventory items that they had previously been forced to rush order when they needed them, wasting time and money, and delaying the vehicle repairs. Stockroom staff had also been spending the equivalent of one day per week, on average, running out to buy parts for urgent needs.

In the end, the project took eleven months, cut inventory by two-thirds, and saved a total of CAD$750,000 annually in recurring costs, plus CAD$1.3 million in "soft savings" (i.e., savings realized in cost avoidance or salaried staff time). These savings do not include the benefits of getting vehicles back on the road faster.

Rapid Improvement Events (RIEs) are used for improvement projects that can be completed over a shorter period of time if the right people are brought together and given a few days to focus on a problem. A good example took place at the province's Department of Finance, which was spending more than CAD$1.3 million annually to borrow money to maintain adequate minimum bank balances for the New Brunswick Regional Health Authorities. After analyzing the situation, the team put together a business case for cutting the size of the minimum bank balances by more than half, saving the province over CAD$720,000 annually in interest costs.

Waste Walk ideas are the smaller everyday improvement opportunities identified directly by front-line employees in the course of their daily work. The Waste Walk training introduces the basic principles of problem identification and waste elimination in a short course of just a few hours. Examples of Waste Walk improvements include the following:

- A staffer at the New River Beach Provincial Park suggested a switch in internet providers that saved CAD$12,500 annually.

- A Service New Brunswick employee suggested sending out certain licenses in smaller envelopes, which saved CAD$70,000 per year, much of which was in postage.

- An employee did an actual walk around one of the district yards at the Department of Transportation and Infrastructure (DTI) and identified a great deal of surplus equipment. As a result, the DTI was able to cancel contracts for CAD$200,000 in new equipment and auction off another CAD$40,000 of excess equipment.

- Another DTI employee pointed out that the department was spending more than CAD$1 million per year outsourcing its archeological work (to ensure public projects were not disturbing potentially valuable or important sites or relics). The employee made a business case to hire a permanent expert for this work. Not only did this save considerable money, but the department was relieved of the extra work of contracting with and managing the consultants.

Daily Management is the approach used by every work team to monitor and improve the way its work is done. On a daily basis, work teams use whiteboards to list problems, capture improvement ideas, and monitor idea implementation. (Front-line idea systems are discussed more in Chapter 8.)

As the program was rolled out, the hard dollar savings grew rapidly: from CAD$3,998,962 in fiscal year 2012–2013 and CAD$11,306,526 in 2013–2014, to CAD$17,545,063 in 2014–2015 and CAD$22,624,884 in 2015–2016. Once confidence in Lean Six Sigma was established and government priorities changed, New Brunswick stopped reporting dollar savings on the Balanced Scorecard and put more emphasis on improving service performance. While the CI program has saved New Brunswick taxpayers hundreds of millions of dollars over the years, its most lasting impact is the province's ongoing ability to improve the efficiency and effectiveness of its government.

Notice the genius in the concept and name of the Formal Management System. There is no specific reference to CI in its name, yet with employee-driven continuous improvement designed into it, CI has simply become part of the way the New Brunswick government manages itself, independent of the political party in power.

By insisting on the new positions, requiring extensive training, and using the Balanced Scorecard to roll down goal-aligned performance metrics, the OSM provided centralized leadership and clear focus to New Brunswick's CI effort. At the same time, because responsibility for the actual improvement efforts is decentralized, each department is able to take on the improvement opportunities most appropriate to meeting its goals.

6

The Top Leader's Role in Creating Front-Line–Driven Improvement

As the New Brunswick story shows, for a large department or organization, front-line–driven improvement means much more than having a bunch of front-line leaders independently improving their units. In addition, it does not mean that improvement is happening *solely* on the front lines. It means that when identifying and solving problems—at whatever level they occur—the organization takes advantage of front-line knowledge. This often includes significant involvement of front-line personnel on high-level problem-solving teams.

Consider the projects at the Moncton Provincial Court to fix the scheduling issues and at the Vehicle Maintenance Agency to reduce the cost of parts inventories and handling. These were big system-level problems. Moncton was the busiest court in the province, and the VMA had operations spread over thirty-one stockrooms. Although both of these improvement teams included managers and professionals, each was also heavily staffed with front-line employees. This merging of the boundary-spanning authority of upper management and the expertise of professional staff, with the practicality and situation-specific knowledge of front-line employees, resulted in solutions that were effective and easy to implement. A less obvious benefit of the front-line involvement was that the solutions to these high-level problems did not need to be "sold" to the front-line workers, because their perspectives were already well represented in the solutions. And, given the additional front-line improvement tools, such as the Waste Walks and Daily Management boards, the initial solutions from the teams could be quickly refined and built upon as part of the normal CI activity.

The attraction of front-line–driven CI is obvious. Put yourself in Minister Blaine Higgs's shoes when he first heard what Jane Washburn had accomplished at Alcool NB Liquor. If such an improvement culture could be created for the entire provincial government, he knew, it could go a long way to solving its financial problems. But how could he transform a large, slow-moving bureaucratic culture into one in which improvement and change were the norm? In the beginning, Washburn herself thought it would be difficult.

Every successful organization-wide CI initiative that we studied began with the actions of the top leaders. Although each initiative seemed to take a different approach, every one of the top leaders followed strategies that incorporated the same four key elements. They

- provided an improvement-oriented vision;

- identified, empowered, and supported a champion to lead their CI initiative;

- got managers at all levels on board; and

- provided the ongoing support and resources needed to make the initiative a success.

In the rest of this chapter, we look at each of these elements in more detail. Although nominally there is a sequential order to these actions, it is important to note that their timing usually overlaps.

Create an Improvement-Oriented Vision

Michael Hancock ran for Mayor of Denver with a vision of improving the performance of city government. Hancock had served on the Denver City Council for eight years, and as he told us, he had learned where the inefficiencies in the city were and whose help he would need to fix them. As he put it: "The real power in government lies with the employees."

"The real power in government
lies with the employees."
—DENVER MAYOR MICHAEL HANCOCK

While campaigning for Mayor, Hancock knew that the city would be facing an $80 million budget shortfall. By the time he took office, he already had a CI initiative mapped out. This initiative, which he named "Peak Performance," was inspired by Baltimore's CitiStat, a data-driven approach that establishes performance goals and metrics and holds middle and upper managers accountable for them. But Hancock went a step further. He put employee involvement front and center in the Peak Performance model. He told us that he wanted to "invest in city employees, train them in how to make government better, faster, and stronger, and empower them to innovate." In a reflective moment, he also told us that he anticipated that the city's CI initiative would be one of his most important legacies.

Shortly after taking office, Hancock established Peak Academy to provide expert CI support and to train employees in CI concepts and tools. (Recall that Stacie Loucks of Denver Licensing relied on Peak Academy for both training and technical support.) Hancock himself was one of the early graduates of the academy's "black belt" training, which included five days of classroom work and required the completion of a workplace improvement project. By the end of his second term in office, over 6,500 employees had gone through either black-belt or green-belt training—literally *half* the city's workforce. Hancock's vision was to make innovation and improvement "the values we govern with" and to embed those values so deeply into the city government's culture that they would remain in place long after he left office.

During one visit, we attended the city government's annual Innovation Fair, in which employees from departments throughout the city set up booths and poster boards to share recent improvements with each other and the general public. The day-long fair took up the large ground-floor atrium of the main municipal building located downtown. Mayor Hancock opened the fair with a heartfelt speech, and then spent several hours touring the exhibits. All city employees were encouraged to come by, and the event was well attended. It closed with an impressive keynote from Ken Miller, a prominent author and expert on government improvement.

Just as Minister Higgs had done with his people in New Brunswick, Mayor Hancock made sure that the vision of front-line–driven improvement was clear to city managers and employees. And he also carefully avoided dictating specific improvements, leaving these to the lower levels, where local realities could be taken into account.

Choose and Empower an Improvement Champion

While doing research for an earlier book on creating high-performance organizations, we had the opportunity to talk with Roger Milliken, CEO of Milliken & Company, about how he transformed his company into one that was front-line driven. At the time, Milliken & Company had one of the best front-line idea systems in the world that was implementing more than a hundred ideas per employee per year. We asked him how he had been able to create such a strong CI culture in his company.

> The biggest challenge for top leaders was to work
> through multiple layers of management to affect
> what was happening at the front-line level.

He told us that it all stemmed from a critical piece of advice given to him by Philip Crosby, one of the leading management gurus of the twentieth century, and the author of the pioneering book *Quality Is Free*. Milliken had hired Crosby to help his company attain world-class quality, and it was clear that this would require a major break with the company's long tradition of top-down management. During a private talk with Milliken, Crosby had advised that

> *If you implement this program, it will represent a radical change in the way you manage and lead people. And you can't lead it by yourself, because you have been managing the company in the same way for forty years.*
>
> *The only way you can change your culture is to find a horse in your organization and challenge him to pull the company forward by leading the transformation in his area. Your job is to put scorecards in place. Create one for everyone on your management team, make sure you review them every four weeks in your policy committee meetings, and let your horse do his work. Let everyone see the results. You are going to have to manage the process, because otherwise your managers will gang up on your horse and kill him and kill you with him. And then nothing will change in your company.*[1]

So Milliken found his "horse," Tom Malone, one of his plant managers. With the CEO's support, Malone was able to transform his operation, and then Milliken & Company as a whole. He eventually became president of the company.

Without exception, the top leaders in our study found such champions to lead their CI initiatives. New Brunswick's Minister Blaine Higgs chose Jane Washburn, Hancock had David Edinger and Scotty Martin (who launched Peak Academy), Arizona's Governor Doug Ducey recruited Rob Woods to set up his Government Transformation Office, York Region had Ted Burley, and Governor Jay Inslee of Washington had Wendy Korthuis-Smith (who set up Results Washington, the state's continuous improvement office). These champions had extensive knowledge of CI techniques and systems and were politically astute. They were strong advocates of front-line–driven improvement and had the emotional intelligence and institutional savvy to pull it off. They were also particularly adept at engineering significant organizational change without antagonizing people (too much).

Get the Leadership Team on Board

It is not a simple matter to build the type of broad-based support from top and middle managers that is needed for front-line–driven improvement. During our study, many managers confided that the level of empowerment they were trying to create required a dramatic break with the top-down approach they had been working with throughout their careers. Other managers found front-line–driven improvement hard to even fathom, and they were hesitant to try it. How could front-line ideas really be such a significant source of improvement? And even if front-line workers could come up with so many ideas, could they be trusted to decide which ones to implement without being self-serving? Because of this widespread skepticism and reluctance, the successful top leaders in our study treated launching CI as a major cultural change initiative.

Earlier, we introduced Jay Galbraith's simple schema for overcoming individual resistance to change. But for large-scale organizational change, where leaders have to work indirectly through layers of other managers, something more is needed. A useful framework in this context is the one developed by Kenneth Benne and Robert Chin, two noted scholars in the field of organizational change.

Benne and Chin's taxonomy classifies change tactics into three distinct categories.[2] The first, *rational-empirical* tactics, make the case for change with logical arguments, data, and analysis. The second category, *normative-re-educative* approaches, includes tactics designed to shift norms and culture by getting people to look at things from a different perspective, usually through education. The third category is *power-coercive* tactics—tactics that use authority or coercion to force compliance. The leaders of the successful organization-wide CI initiatives typically used strategies blending all three types of tactics. And when they did use power-coercive tactics, it was with a light hand.

Anticipating widespread skepticism and reluctance, the successful top leaders treated launching organization-wide front-line–driven improvement as a major cultural change initiative.

When New Brunswick's Finance Minister Higgs had Jane Washburn present the results of her improvement program at Alcool NB Liquor to the deputy ministers, he was employing a rational-empirical tactic. They were all looking for ways to deal with budget cuts, so it was easy for them to grasp intellectually the advantages of the new approach. Once the deputy ministers accepted the concept, they and their leadership teams were all given extensive training, a normative-re-educative tactic. Higgs subtly used a power-coercive tactic by modifying something that was already routine for department heads—accountability for performance. The difference was that during their quarterly meetings with their boss, the Clerk of the Executive Council, they now had to address their departments'

CI performance through the Balanced Scorecard metrics tracked by Jane Washburn's office.

Demonstrate Highly Visible Ongoing Support

The public actions of top government leaders are highly visible. Their managers and employees pay attention to what they say and even closer attention to what they do. Top leaders are in unique positions to champion CI, and their unwavering support is critical to building and sustaining an organization-wide front-line–driven improvement culture.

Mayor Hancock's support for CI was never in doubt. It was a central theme of his campaign and the focus of many of his early actions. His support never wavered. He never missed an opportunity to extol the improvements made by city employees, and he made a point of attending Peak Academy black-belt certification ceremonies and the annual Innovation Fair. On the website for the mayor's office, there was a prominent link to the Peak Performance webpage, which displayed city-level performance metrics, acted as the portal to CI resources and training, had links to the Peak Academy blog, and listed many examples of improvements. City managers and employees always knew where Hancock stood on employee-driven CI.

Every year, Governor Inslee delivered the opening keynote at the Washington State Government Lean Transformation Conference—the largest and longest-running conference on government CI in the world. And every month he held a televised Results Review meeting. On a rotating basis, each meeting focused on one of the state's five strategic priorities. During the meeting, department heads reported on their progress toward the goals set for that month's strategic priority. After each report, the governor probed into performance issues and led a discussion about how further progress could be made. Recordings of all past Results Reviews, as well as a dashboard summarizing the state's performance on all five of the governor's priorities and their corresponding sub-goals, were publicly available on the Results Washington website.

Online performance dashboards were frequently used by the top elected officials or political appointees we studied. These public-facing websites allowed citizens easy access to what was often detailed performance information and gave them the means to track the improvement in their government's performance. These dashboards served several purposes. First, they telegraphed that performance improvement was important to top leadership. Second, they showed which *aspects* of performance were most important to these leaders. And third, they instilled accountability for improvement throughout the organization—for the top elected official and the leadership team, as well as the department leaders whose results were displayed. The dashboards also provided top leaders with a high-level view of the effects of CI, which allowed them to drill down and intervene wherever their help was needed.

7

Creating the Improvement Infrastructure and Launching the Initiative

t takes much more than good intentions and executive edicts to create an organization-wide culture of front-line–driven improvement. It requires a well-thought-through system and support infrastructure. In this chapter, we discuss the main elements of this infrastructure, starting with a group of CI experts led by the CI champion we discussed in the last chapter.

Establish an Office of Improvement Expertise

Immediately upon being assigned responsibility for New Brunswick's CI initiative, Jane Washburn began assembling a group of experts to provide the training, support, and oversight needed for the upcoming effort. This group eventually became the Office of Strategy Management (OSM).

Every successful organization-wide CI initiative that we studied started by setting up such a support office staffed with a team of experts. Although they might occasionally facilitate larger and more complex improvement projects, these experts were *not* charged with making improvements themselves, but with helping *others* across the organization build their own improvement capability. The CI offices were surprisingly small, but by focusing their efforts on program development, training, and coaching, they were able to leverage their expertise to have a huge impact. For example, the five thousand employees in York Region were well served by a CI office of just two people.

It can be tempting to let the experts in the CI group undertake most of the improvements themselves. This mistake explained why several of the attempts at organization-wide CI that we studied were so short-lived. Relying on a team of experts to make most of the improvements does get the initiative off to a quick start and can produce good results for a while—more than enough to justify the team's costs. But such an approach foregoes the far greater impact possible when everyone is engaged in making improvements.

> When CI is the exclusive domain of the "experts," the organization foregoes the far greater impact possible when everyone is engaged in making improvements.

In the successful initiatives, the CI support offices were strategically placed in their organizations' hierarchies. They were embedded in positions of power as permanent parts of the machinery of government, and care was taken not to identify them with a particular partisan agenda or political leader. If the improvement initiatives had been viewed as political, they might well have been subject to elimination by the next administration. This was the thinking behind having New Brunswick's OSM report directly to the top civil-service administrator. It subsequently thrived through three changes in the province's political leadership. Likewise, Denver's Peak Academy was housed in the Finance department, perhaps the most powerful department in the city's government.

British Prime Minister Tony Blair, on the other hand, set up his Delivery Unit as an independent group within the prime minister's office and tied it closely to himself personally as part of his political agenda to improve government. Although this gave the unit great clout while Blair was in power, and he no doubt benefited from being seen as a champion of efficient government, it was shut down not long after he left office.

Design the Organization's Improvement System

Jane Washburn started her job as head of New Brunswick's CI initiative with extensive knowledge of Lean Six Sigma. She had worked with it in the private sector at J. D. Irving, and she had implemented it at Alcool NB Liquor. But the provincial government was an entirely different animal. Washburn needed to creatively modify the approach and deployment for a much more complicated setting.

There are many approaches to CI, and countless variants of each of these. And the wide variety of options was reflected in the organizations in our study. While these approaches all shared the goal of continuous improvement, each had its own language, perspective, and associated techniques. In practice, the approach taken depended to some extent upon the training and experience of the experts in the CI office, but mostly on the purposes of the programs being designed. And these purposes were surprisingly varied. For example:

- The Lean Everyday Ideas system at the Colorado Department of Transportation (CDOT) was designed to capture front-line ideas that improve safety, boost productivity, and reduce costs from almost three hundred patrols (i.e., road crews) and engineering offices spread around the state and replicate them quickly in the other units that could use them.

- The Lean Six Sigma initiative in New Brunswick was started to mitigate a severe financial crisis. Its primary improvement activity targeted cost-savings, and success was measured in dollars.

■ When Denmark's MindLab was tasked with helping the national government create better policies, the critical element was understanding how the policies worked in practice and how they impacted people and their behavior. To this end, MindLab deployed a method based on design-thinking and ethnographic studies to provide policymakers with insights into the consequences of their policies. (More on this in Chapter 15.)

■ With 95 percent of its budget going to contractors, Highways England (HE), the government organization responsible for all the major motorways in England, could only improve if it could get its *contractors* to improve. It focused its CI initiative on getting its contractors to adopt lean construction techniques and to share their improvements with each other so that HE benefitted across its entire supply chain. In other words, it turned its supply chain into a giant transorganizational learning network. (More on this in Chapter 13.)

■ The goal of York regional government was to promote mass front-line engagement in problem solving. As such, it developed some tools designed specifically for this purpose: The York Den (similar to *Shark Tank*), crowdsourcing campaigns, and a modified set of creativity tools that could be used for large-group creative problem solving.

None of these CI systems, nor any of the other successful systems we studied, ever stood still. They evolved quickly as experience was gained, approaches were refined, new kinds of problems were encountered, and priorities shifted. Over time, they morphed into their own unique hybrid variant. Considering this, perhaps the most important thing that selecting an initial CI approach provides is a set of techniques, a common improvement vocabulary, and a place to start.

Launch the Improvement System

To get an organization-wide CI initiative started quickly, it might be tempting to launch it with some fanfare and a "shotgun" start—that is, where the entire organization starts at the same time. None of the successful organizations we studied did this. They all deployed their programs in a deliberate and measured way, gradually expanding the number of units involved. New Brunswick, for example, spread its launch over a three-year period, and then incrementally added further CI components over the following three years.

> To get started quickly, it might be tempting to launch an organization-wide CI initiative where everyone starts at the same time. But it is far better to launch in a deliberate and measured way, gradually expanding the number of units involved.

A measured launch has two advantages. First, starting off small allows the CI office to spot any aspects of the program that are not working well and fix them quickly before the broader rollout makes changes more difficult. One tactic for flagging these kinds of problems is to encourage the early adopters to complain loudly whenever they encounter issues with the program.

The other reason for a measured launch is that a small CI group can support only a limited number of units in their launch phase at any one time. It takes resources to train employees in CI techniques and give them the coaching and expert support they need. If the capacity of the CI group is exceeded, it will not be able to adequately support all the launching units, and the effort will be much less likely to succeed.

Even a measured launch can outstrip the support capacity of a small CI group. Some of the organizations in our study had tens of thousands of employees. In these cases, the organizations brought in outside trainers and consultants whose work was carefully coordinated by the central CI offices. The goal was knowledge transfer, and care was taken to avoid the CI initiative becoming dependent on outside consultants.

One particularly effective variation of the measured launch, which we encountered a number of times, is what Brian Elms, former director of Denver's Peak Academy, described as building a "coalition of the willing." For the first several years, the city government did not mandate that any managers adopt CI. Managers could freely choose to participate or not. But when they did, Peak Academy gave them all the training and support they needed to be successful.

The coalition of the willing strategy has several advantages. Because it deals with only willing managers, it neatly sidesteps the problem of having to overcome management resistance. And when managers who have volunteered to adopt CI encounter the inevitable "teething pains" of the new initiative, they are more invested in overcoming the underlying issues. This increases the chances of early success, which in turn provides more evidence of CI's potential to managers who have yet to join the coalition. The WSP garage was one such early success for Results Washington, and the state used that success very persuasively. The first two annual Washington State Government Lean Transformation Conferences showcased a converted patrol cruiser with a team of installers standing by to share their story. In both years, attendees rated the patrol car exhibit as one of the most memorable and useful aspects of the conference.

Another benefit of the coalition of the willing approach is that the early adopters frequently become a cadre of experienced and enthusiastic CI experts who will encourage their peers to join the initiative, and help them when they do. This significantly leverages the resources of the CI office.

Over time, as more managers join the coalition, the laggards find it increasingly difficult to hold out. Those that do often find themselves gradually being left behind as their career opportunities and influence erode.

Integrate Improvement into Everyday Work Routines

For a CI effort to take hold and be sustainable, it must become a regular part of the organization's work. In practice, this means that leaders must ensure that CI is integrated into the processes, systems, and policies that determine how everyday work gets done. In the organizations we studied, most often this was more a matter of making minor changes to existing systems and processes than it was about creating anything new. Without articulating it as such, the CI offices made use of the principle of *minimal intervention,* which states that any change in how an organization works is much more likely to be accepted if it minimally intervenes in how things are *already done.* In other words, if existing systems or processes could be tweaked to perform whatever new CI-related tasks were needed, the organizations did so instead of creating entirely new systems. The less that people are required to modify their behavior, the more easily they will accept change.

The leaders in our study took special care to align two elements for CI: 1) the focus of the improvement effort and 2) holding managers accountable for improvement activity.

Any change is much more likely to be accepted if it minimally intervenes in how things are already done.

Focusing Improvement Efforts

Any competent leader formulates direction and goals that are strategic and tied to an overarching vision. But the leaders in our study went further: they then focused their organizations' considerable improvement capabilities on these goals. From his first day in office, Denver's Mayor Hancock emphasized continuous improvement as the best way to achieve his strategic priorities: Children, Growth, Public Safety, Mobility, and the Social Safety Net. Washington State's Governor Inslee also articulated five priority areas: World Class Education; Prosperous Economy; Sustainable Energy and Clean Environment; Healthy and Safe Communities; and Efficient, Effective, and Accountable Government. In both cases, these high-level priorities were translated into outcome measures that were then tracked on publicly facing dashboards in order to communicate these leaders' priorities and track progress toward achieving them.

But the top leaders in our study did more than simply signal their priorities and expect that everyone would fall into line. They put in place systems to link their top-level goals to front-line metrics, and hence to front-line *action*. New Brunswick did this with a Balanced Scorecard approach. Recall that its goal-setting process began with the political party in power articulating its top priorities, which were then cascaded down through the various departments all the way to front-line units. While this process gives the impression of tightly aligned organizational goals, the reality is that the alignment is, and should be, a bit looser. Front-line leaders need the latitude to take on problems that they see as important at their level.

We saw how this loose linkage played out in New Brunswick while studying a Lean Six Sigma project that dramatically increased student literacy levels at the Soleil Levant primary school near Moncton in New Brunswick. (The full story is in Chapter 10.) Throughout our visit we were accompanied by a Lean Six Sigma master black belt from the Department of Education in Fredericton (the capital). At one point, we met with Monique Boudreau, the regional director of Francophone Sud, the school district where Soleil Levant is located. In our discussion, she detailed the four major focus goals of her district. Hearing the list, the black belt commented, "I'm glad that two of your four goals are nicely aligned with our province-level goals."

This loose-tight linkage between top-level vision and front-line realities is essential for attaining operational excellence.

Instilling Accountability for Improvement

In different ways and at different rates, the organization-wide initiatives in our study incorporated accountability for CI into annual reviews, performance reports, merit increases, and promotion criteria. For the most part, this was relatively straightforward and was consistent with the principle of minimal intervention. Many performance reviews already include elements that can be easily modified, or even directly interpreted, to cover CI contributions.

The accountability element that seemed to have the greatest long-term impact was including CI performance in promotion criteria. This practice played out in one way or another in most of the high-performing government organizations we studied. In the York regional government, for example, experience as an ILab facilitator (more on ILab in Chapter 12) was seen as a career enhancer. Facilitating ILab improvement workshops was a high-visibility demonstration of leadership potential and showed the commitment to improvement that top leaders valued in their managers. Other organizations explicitly include CI performance as part of their promotion criteria. This not only sends a strong signal about what is important for advancement, but over time, populates the ranks of management with improvement-oriented leaders.

PART 3

A Full Set of Problem-Solving Approaches for a Wide Spectrum of Issues

The tools and techniques associated with CI play a vital role in creating an improvement culture and giving people the capability to solve many problems they otherwise could not. Equally important, because most CI problem solving is *team* based, having everyone trained in the same set of tools and techniques provides them with a common language of improvement, as well as a common framework with which to identify, understand, and solve problems. The training people get in these tools also provides the technical foundation for creating an improvement culture.

Improvement opportunities come in all sizes, types, and levels of complexity. They range from simple ideas that can be implemented quickly by front-line employees, to complex cross-functional issues that require considerable analytical work and resources to resolve. As such, an organization must have a full range of problem-solving approaches that covers the spectrum of issues it will face.

The effective CI initiatives in our study covered this spectrum with approaches that addressed at least three different levels of problems. In Part 3 we discuss common approaches for each of these levels. Chapter 8 is about systems to handle large numbers of (usually small) front-line improvement ideas. Chapter 9 is about medium-size process-level problems that can be solved by assembling a small group of the right people and providing them with a little time and some resources. Chapter 10 is about approaches for large, complex, systems-level issues that take significant amounts of time, expertise, resources, and clout to resolve. In Chapter 11, we show how the British Royal Mint has deployed a full spectrum of improvement approaches that has given it the capability to make the most difficult coins in the world to counterfeit.

A SPECIAL NOTE. Many CI experts put so much emphasis on tools and techniques that it is easy to lose sight of the fact that creating a successful improvement initiative is actually more about leadership and change management. Our goal is to avoid the "tools morass" and to communicate the importance of having a full spectrum of problem-solving capability, rather than suggest specific tools or provide detailed discussions of how they work. Many books, consultants, classes, and videos are readily available to help you with that. Learning the tools and techniques is the easiest part of the CI journey.

8

Systems for Getting and Handling Large Numbers of Small Front-Line Ideas

Today, the best idea systems in the world routinely implement twenty, fifty, or even a hundred ideas per employee per year. Although these high-performing systems may look very different, they all operate on the same underlying principles. They are simple, rapid, and efficient. They are also *team based*, with ideas being discussed, decided on, and largely implemented by the front-line employees themselves. A "typical" system works as follows. People bring problems and improvement ideas to regular meetings of their work teams. If the underlying problem is easily understood and someone has a simple solution that is obviously worth trying, the team quickly agrees upon it and assigns implementation responsibility to a team member, usually the person who came up with the idea. If the underlying problem is not fully understood, or the proposed solution could be improved, the team discusses the issues involved and brings its collective wisdom into play. Perhaps the original idea is modified, perhaps the team comes up with a completely different idea, or perhaps the problem requires further investigation. The goal is to handle as many ideas as possible rapidly and at the local level.

When an idea requires higher-level approval, help from support departments, resources beyond those available to the team to implement, or working with other units, it is escalated to the appropriate higher authority. When an idea is escalated, it should be fully documented, including the rationale for it, so management has all the pertinent information needed to make an informed decision quickly and easily.

The best idea systems in the world routinely implement twenty, fifty, or even a hundred ideas per employee per year. They are team based, with ideas being discussed, decided on, and largely implemented by the front-line employees themselves.

Despite using similar underlying processes, individual idea systems may differ considerably depending on their goals and organizational settings. To demonstrate how contextual differences can result in very different approaches, we contrast the systems of two different states, both in their departments of transportation, and both highly effective at what they are designed to do. The first is in an office setting at a branch of the Motor Vehicles Division (MVD), which is part of the Arizona Department of Transportation (ADOT). It comes with an informative back story, which we use to set the stage. The second system, at the Colorado Department of Transportation (CDOT) is highly decentralized and designed to get ideas from work crews and staff spread throughout the state.

Arizona's Huddle-Board System

For many citizens of Arizona, dealing with the MVD—for such things as driver's licenses, vehicle registrations, titles, and license plates—was extremely unpleasant. The service was poor, the staff was overloaded, and the wait times were measured in hours. With forty-five locations around the state, the MVD was the face of the government for most people. When Eric Jorgensen was appointed director of the MVD in 2015, he was given a mandate: fix the mess.

The CI initiative that Jorgensen launched was part of an ambitious plan by Governor Doug Ducey to create a lean transformation across state government. Early in his first term, Ducey had visited the Department of Environment Quality (ADEQ), an early adopter of lean during Governor Jan Brewer's administration. When he saw what they were doing, he asked, "Why can't we do this everywhere in state government?"

The governor set up the Government Transformation Office, headed by Rob Woods, to facilitate and oversee the lean effort, which the state named the Arizona Management System (AMS). The approach taken to get it going was called "Mile Wide, Mile Deep." The *Mile Wide* component involved training every state employee in lean, starting with top leadership and rolling the training down by tiers until it reached the front lines three years later. The *Mile Deep* aspect required each department to choose two small but critical units in which to fully implement lean. The idea was to learn from these efforts, and showcase them, in order to help with the broader deployment of lean. ADOT selected as one of its Mile Deep experiments the 51st Avenue MVD service center, which had the worst reputation of all its service centers. If lean could make a difference there, it could work anywhere.

The 51st Avenue service center deserved its poor reputation. It was always jammed with people, the noise was deafening, and the waiting-room environment was chaotic. Two separate automated numerical queueing systems, one for the photograph line and one for all other transactions, added to the confusion for people trying to get service. The average wait time was seventy-three minutes, with waits of more than three hours during peak periods.

Because people came prepared for long waits, many brought their pets, children, and elderly parents that they could not leave alone at home for extended periods. They brought food, drink, and reading material. They listened to music and watched movies on their devices. Homeless people moved in during the day for relief from the intense Arizona heat. They used the bathrooms for "sink showers," leaving water all over the floor. Facility maintenance costs were extremely high, as the facilities department was constantly being called to make repairs or remove graffiti. And managers were spending inordinate amounts of time writing up and filing incident reports.

When customers arrived, they checked in at the information desk, where they were given a number through the automated queuing system. When their number was called, they had three minutes to get to the assigned window. But people would often miss the announcements. Because of the long waits, they might be watching a movie, listening to music, engrossed in a book, or simply not hear the announcement over all the noise. This led to delays and some forty to fifty missed numbers per day.

Another problem arose because the automated system cycled through only fifty numbers. With the long lines, when a number was called, often two people would show up at the window! The customer service representative (CSR) would have to look at the time stamps and explain to one party that they still had fifty customers ahead of them.

The automated queuing system was only one of many problems. For example, on almost a daily basis, the credentials printer would break down, and it would take thirty minutes or so to fix. In that time, forty to fifty people would stack up waiting for their licenses, titles, or other legal documents to be printed.

In March 2016, the Mile Deep effort began at the 51st Avenue Center. The Deep Dive team (as it was called) consisted of an office manager, two supervisors from other offices, five CSRs, two consultants from Honsha (the consulting company assigned to the MVD), a person from the MVD's central office of CI, and a person from Arizona General Services (the centralized business services department). In addition, floating representatives from departments such as IT and facilities participated as needed. The team members met and worked two days per week for the first six months, and one day a week thereafter. They quickly realized that the total wait times were longer than had been reported. The branch had been measuring times for only *part* of the service process.

The team began by setting what it saw as an appropriate target—customers should be able to take an hour off work and get their business done. Allowing for a fifteen-minute commute each way, this meant that a customer had to be served within thirty minutes from the time they walked into the center.

Despite the team making some good initial progress, wait times remained stubbornly high. A big contributor to the problem was the dead time between serving customers. It took an average of two minutes for the next customer to arrive at the window once their number was called.

Then one day, while the team was meeting at the center, the automated queuing system went down. The effect was dramatic. The CSRs went into manual mode, marshaled the customers into a single line with a CSR acting as dispatcher. The room became orderly and quiet. Most of the Deep Dive team members, except the ones who were CSRs, were baffled. Things were moving *much* faster. This is when the outside members of the team realized that the automatic queuing system was a big part of the problem, and the manual backup procedure was far superior. Because everyone was in a single line, as they approached their turn, they were ready to move quickly to the next open CSR. The delay between servicing customers dropped to practically zero, and overall wait times fell dramatically.

The discussion that followed between the Deep Dive team members and the CSRs was enlightening. The CSRs had long known about the problems with the automatic queuing system—they had been begging to get rid of it for years. It was also clear from the discussion that the lean initiative had been overlooking a major source of improvement ideas. As Kismet Weiss, Continuous Improvement Leader at ADOT, put it, "That was probably the biggest change for us on our [lean] journey. We finally acknowledged that the people doing the work knew the problems better than we did."

> The biggest lesson learned by ADOT on its lean journey was that the people doing the work understood the problems better than management did.

After that, the improvement effort quickly pivoted to put more emphasis on front-line ideas and to getting the huddle-board process (the front-line idea system component of the AMS) up and running. Wait times started to drop again. As Weiss put it, "Our people wanted something different, and this [the huddle-board process] gave them something different in a way that empowered them to make changes and decisions." Today, at the 51st Avenue Center, 75 percent of customers are served and out the door in under fifteen minutes. The service is so quick that chairs are no longer needed in the lobby and most have been removed. And maintenance costs have been greatly reduced, as customers spend little time in the center and homeless people no longer use it as a hangout.

The Mile Deep project at the 51st Avenue Center proved that the lean concept worked well, even in the most trying of settings. But more importantly, it demonstrated to management the critical role of front-line involvement in CI.

The ADOT huddle-board process works as follows. Each work team has a board where its members post problems and ideas. During the team's daily "huddle," these problems and ideas are discussed. Decisions are made, and actions to be taken are assigned and posted on the board for follow-up at subsequent huddles. Once an idea is implemented, it is uploaded into a central database. Overall progress on key metrics is also tracked on the board.

The huddle boards at the front-line level are linked to a series of tiered huddle boards at higher levels. In this way, if a problem or idea at one level needs higher-level support or authority, it is escalated to the next higher board, and so on until it reaches a level that has the resources and authority needed to take action. At the same time, key concerns that are identified at a higher level but that need to be addressed at a lower level can be cascaded back down through the tiered board system.

ADOT's huddle-board process has built-in accountability. Everyone is expected to participate, but the exact form of accountability is left up to the individual units. For example, at the time we were studying the 51st Avenue Center, it had a formal participation goal of one implemented idea from each of its employees every month.

Colorado Department of Transportation's Lean Everyday Ideas System

The Colorado Department of Transportation (CDOT) is responsible for constructing and maintaining the state's highways, controlling traffic and enhancing safety, developing public transit, clearing snow and ice, and even running one of the state's smaller airports. Its employees are spread across the state, with 221 front-line "patrols" (of four to six employees each) and 53 "engineering residences" (of ten to twelve employees each), plus regional offices and the central operations in Denver. Each patrol and engineering residence is responsible for specified routine work in its designated area. Some of the patrols are quite isolated, with their management as far as fifty miles away. CDOT's Lean Everyday Ideas program, which is led by the Office of Process Improvement in Denver, captures, processes, and shares the improvement ideas from this geographically diverse mix of employees.

Lean Everyday Ideas uses a web-based portal to facilitate the gathering and processing of front-line ideas.[1] Employees can access the smartphone-friendly website from anywhere, so simple ideas can be entered even while patrol workers are out on the job. When accessing the site, employees are given the choice of two buttons: "I Fixed It" or "I Suggest." Most ideas go to the "I Fixed It" part, which captures ideas that have already been implemented to solve a problem. In submitting an idea, the employee explains the problem, describes the idea (often including photos), and lays out the resulting performance improvement. Most ideas from patrol employees are discussed, developed, and implemented by the entire patrol, with everyone sharing credit. The "I Suggest" button is for problems that cannot be solved at the local level, that need higher-level authority, or that require specialized knowledge or skills.

Submitted ideas are reviewed by staff at the Office of Process Improvement in Denver. The "I Suggest" ideas are forwarded to a person who can follow through on them, and the "I Fixed It" ideas are reviewed to determine which ones can be used by other patrols or groups. If an idea is replicable, an *idea card* is created. Idea cards are not physical cards, but pages on a web site that describe the improvement and its advantages and that provide all the information needed for others to duplicate it.[2] Table 8.1 lists a small sample of the ideas on the website.

Table 8.1. Implemented Ideas from CDOT

1	Old speed limit sign covers (used for temporary speed limit changes) were made of plywood and frequently blew off in the wind, endangering cars. A rollup hood–type cover was invented that is easy to install and does not blow off.
2	A new cart design (costing less than $200 to make) reduced the work involved in mounting and removing a wing plow (the plow extension on the side of a plow truck) from two hours for two employees, to six minutes for one employee, with greatly improved safety.
3	An improved de-icer connection between storage tanks and the trucks eliminated roughly two gallons of spillage each time a truck was filled with de-icer.
4	Traditionally, CDOT used magnesium chloride as the base for its de-icing fluids. A group of employees at the Southwestern Colorado site developed a system to generate salt brine, which saved $394,000 in just the first year.
5	Instead of cleaning delineators (steel posts with reflectors) on state highways with buckets and brushes, workers figured out how to use a pump already on the trucks to create a high-pressure spray cleaner so they will no longer have to get out of the truck. This saved major amounts of time, and resulted in a more effective and safer cleaning process. Cost: $40 per truck.

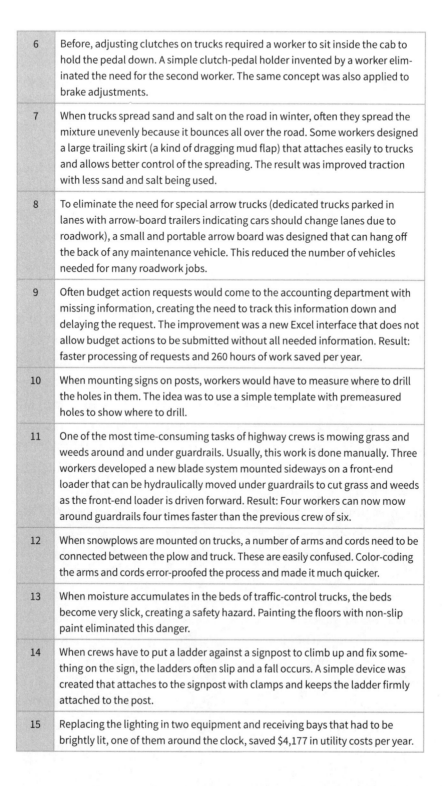

6	Before, adjusting clutches on trucks required a worker to sit inside the cab to hold the pedal down. A simple clutch-pedal holder invented by a worker eliminated the need for the second worker. The same concept was also applied to brake adjustments.
7	When trucks spread sand and salt on the road in winter, often they spread the mixture unevenly because it bounces all over the road. Some workers designed a large trailing skirt (a kind of dragging mud flap) that attaches easily to trucks and allows better control of the spreading. The result was improved traction with less sand and salt being used.
8	To eliminate the need for special arrow trucks (dedicated trucks parked in lanes with arrow-board trailers indicating cars should change lanes due to roadwork), a small and portable arrow board was designed that can hang off the back of any maintenance vehicle. This reduced the number of vehicles needed for many roadwork jobs.
9	Often budget action requests would come to the accounting department with missing information, creating the need to track this information down and delaying the request. The improvement was a new Excel interface that does not allow budget actions to be submitted without all needed information. Result: faster processing of requests and 260 hours of work saved per year.
10	When mounting signs on posts, workers would have to measure where to drill the holes in them. The idea was to use a simple template with premeasured holes to show where to drill.
11	One of the most time-consuming tasks of highway crews is mowing grass and weeds around and under guardrails. Usually, this work is done manually. Three workers developed a new blade system mounted sideways on a front-end loader that can be hydraulically moved under guardrails to cut grass and weeds as the front-end loader is driven forward. Result: Four workers can now mow around guardrails four times faster than the previous crew of six.
12	When snowplows are mounted on trucks, a number of arms and cords need to be connected between the plow and truck. These are easily confused. Color-coding the arms and cords error-proofed the process and made it much quicker.
13	When moisture accumulates in the beds of traffic-control trucks, the beds become very slick, creating a safety hazard. Painting the floors with non-slip paint eliminated this danger.
14	When crews have to put a ladder against a signpost to climb up and fix something on the sign, the ladders often slip and a fall occurs. A simple device was created that attaches to the signpost with clamps and keeps the ladder firmly attached to the post.
15	Replacing the lighting in two equipment and receiving bays that had to be brightly lit, one of them around the clock, saved $4,177 in utility costs per year.

The CDOT system is designed not just to gather ideas, but to *replicate* them. Notice how all the ideas in Table 8.1 are widely applicable. While such ideas made a worthwhile contribution to the patrols or job sites where they were first used, their impact was greatly multiplied when they were adopted by other patrols and engineering residences. In addition, the idea card website is public facing and is monitored by local and state departments of transportation across the United States, as well as departments of transportation in a number of other countries. It would be interesting to know the number of times each of CDOT's front-line ideas has been replicated globally.

When Governor Hickenlooper reached his term limit in 2019, and a new administration took office, Gary Vansuch, Director of the Office of Process Improvement, briefed the newly appointed Executive Director of Transportation Shoshana Lew on the Lean Everyday Ideas program. She got so excited by its results that she wanted to "plow" some of its savings back into the program. She set up a contest in which the patrol that submitted the best idea would win a new snowplow truck (worth about $250,000). When the announcement came out, the engineers asked if they could participate in the contest as well. They were allowed to, but if they won, they were told they would have to gift the new truck to one of the patrols. A few months later, when safety statistics moved a tick in the wrong direction for the first time in many years, a similar statewide competition was launched for the best safety ideas.

Unlike the huddle-board system at Arizona's 51st Avenue MVD Center, participation in CDOT's idea system is voluntary. While leaders encourage, welcome, and celebrate ideas, there are no direct consequences for managers or employees who choose not to participate. But people do participate, and very actively, because they benefit from it. Front-line workers use the idea system to make their jobs easier, safer, and more productive. They also get the satisfaction of improving the work for their colleagues and helping to build a CDOT they can be proud to work for. And given that employees are pointing out ways to improve their unit's performance, what manager wouldn't want to keep their ideas coming? After all, they are only making management look good.

In 2018, the Lean Everyday Ideas system was a finalist for the Innovations in American Government award from the Ash Center for Democratic Governance and Innovation at the Harvard Kennedy School. In 2020, it was the North American winner of the Innovation in the Workplace award from *Inspiring Workplaces.*

The Dangerous Temptation of Suggestion-Box Thinking

Although there are many ways to go after front-line ideas, there is one critically important caveat: *avoid suggestion-box thinking.* Suggestion boxes were first introduced in industry more than 140 years ago. Today, the suggestion-box approach, usually in an online manifestation, remains the first thing managers think of for gathering front-line ideas, and it is by far the most widely used method for doing so. In fact, a great many managers that we encounter aren't even aware of any other way to get employee ideas! Although suggestion boxes—whether physical or dressed up as sophisticated online portals—will get some ideas, the ideas are generally so few and of such poor quality that it hardly makes the investment of management time worthwhile.

Thinking that managers know best, and need to approve every idea, creates a huge bottleneck in the flow of ideas because managers have neither the situation-specific knowledge nor the time to evaluate very many of them.

The essence of suggestion-box thinking is that managers know best and that every idea needs to be evaluated and approved by a manager. This creates a huge bottleneck in the flow of ideas because managers have neither the situation-specific knowledge nor the time to evaluate very many of them. To credibly evaluate many front-line ideas, managers must first familiarize themselves with the details of the underlying problem and then assess the specifics (cost, time, and feasibility) of the proposed solution. And even then, they would still not understand a lot of the ideas and their rationales as well as the front-line employees involved. The time and effort required for management to evaluate ideas is why some organizations with suggestion-box-type systems put a minimum size—say $1,000 in cost savings—on ideas that will be considered.

Quite a few managers whose organizations use the suggestion-box approach have confessed to us that given their workloads, by necessity they give low priority to evaluating ideas. At one federal agency we studied, the suggestion system manager told us that his biggest problem was tracking down retirees to inform them of the final disposition of their ideas and any rewards due to them under federal law. A number of the ideas in the system had been "under evaluation" by managers for more than a decade! At one military base we worked at, when we asked about the base's suggestion box, it turned out that it had not been opened in years, as no one had responsibility for it. In fact, no one even knew where the key for it was. When workers don't hear back about their ideas in a timely manner, they feel (with good reason) that management isn't listening to them and quickly become disillusioned with the process.

A high-performing idea system is the anchor of any front-line–driven CI initiative. To learn more about such systems and how to implement them, we recommend our books *Ideas Are Free* and *The Idea-Driven Organization*.

9

Dealing with Mid-Level
Process Problems

I n the late 1980s, Shigeo Shingo, the codeveloper of the Toyota Production System, gave a talk at the University of Massachusetts. A
businessperson in the audience asked him what he thought was the
most important thing that managers needed to work on. "Process
improvement," Shingo replied. "And most managers really don't
understand its importance or how to go about it."

In the decades since Dr. Shingo's comment, process improvement
may have become part of the vocabulary of management, but it is not
as widely practiced as it should be, in either the public or private sectors. As a result, most organizations still operate far less efficiently
and effectively than they could.

This chapter deals with methods for making mid-level process
improvements. These approaches are applicable to any kind of problem that can be solved by getting the right people together (i.e., the
critical stakeholders and others who understand the issues), giving
them a little time and some resources, and following a structured
problem-solving approach.

Process Charting

Before a process can be improved, it must be understood. It needs to be defined and documented, which is most often done with some kind of process flowchart. The flowchart is a step-by-step listing of the individual operations that make up the overall process. It can be a physical chart, with boxes and arrows, or it might be spelled out as a written procedure.

The concept was first articulated by Frank and Lillian Gilbreth, two of the pioneers of time and motion study, in their classic 1921 paper "Process Charts." In it, they wrote:

> *The process chart is a device for visualizing a process as a means of improving it. Every detail of a process is more or less affected by every other detail; therefore the entire process must be presented in such form that it can be visualized all at once before any changes are made in any of its subdivisions. In any subdivision of the process under examination, any changes made without due consideration of all the decisions and all the motions that precede and follow that subdivision will often be found unsuited to the ultimate plan of operation.[1]*

In its most basic form, a flowchart is an ordinal linkage of the various operations (or steps) involved in a process. Since the Gilbreths' first process flowcharts a century ago, many variants and refinements have been introduced. Our goal here is to give a brief overview of the concept and how to apply it. There are plenty of resources available for learning more about the technique.

A process flowchart lays out the process as a whole, which makes it easier to identify bottlenecks and improvement opportunities. For example, it shows when work crosses departmental or functional boundaries, or when it is handed off from one person to another. These are places to look for potential miscommunication and other mistakes in order to prevent them. A process-level view also helps to identify the improvement opportunities with the greatest potential impact. Without a process-level view, it is easy to waste time and resources on local improvements that will have little impact on overall performance. It can also lead to improving one operation in a way that creates bigger problems for other operations.

It is important to keep the process flowchart as simple as practical so staff members don't get lost in the intricacies of the tool or get overwhelmed by the details in the chart—in short, so they don't miss the forest for the trees. The trick is to choose the right level of analysis with which to look at the process.

Process flowcharts are often diagrams with different geometric shapes representing the different types of operation. However, it is generally easiest to start the improvement exercise by laying out the operations in the process on a spreadsheet. A simple format that we often use in our work is a five-column spreadsheet:

- Column 1 is the number of the step: 1, 2, 3 etc.

- Column 2 is a brief description of the step itself.

- Column 3 is a list of the pain points and problems that can happen with this step.

- Column 4 is a list of any improvement ideas the team has gathered for this step.

- Column 5 is what the dream would be for that operation—ideally, how could it work?

It is astonishing how many ideas can come out of a simple process-charting exercise with the right people in the room. Remember how in Chapter 2, the WSP garage installers identified fifty-three improvement opportunities when they charted their process during their Boeing training course?

Structured Problem-Solving Methods

It is surprisingly easy, when improving a process or working on problems of even modest complexity, to make a number of common mistakes. These include not getting good data; solving the wrong problem; jumping quickly to a bad solution; failing to get to the root cause of the problem; not fully implementing your solution; and not monitoring your solution post-implementation to make sure it is working and being used. This is where some form of structured problem-solving technique comes into play. Although there are many such approaches, they mostly follow a step-by-step process that provides a team with a common playbook to help avoid the most frequent mistakes.

For the mid-level problems we are discussing in this chapter, the two most frequently used techniques we found in use were the Rapid Improvement Event (RIE) and the A3 method. Both are highly versatile and are typically used in combination with other CI techniques. In the remainder of this chapter, we describe these techniques and give examples of the kinds of problems they can help solve.

> Mid-level problem-solving approaches are applicable to any kind of problem that can be solved by getting the right people together, giving them a little time and some resources, and following a structured problem-solving approach.

The Rapid Improvement Event

The Rapid Improvement Event (RIE), originally known as a *kaizen blitz* or a *kaizen event* (*kaizen* is Japanese for "improvement"), was developed half a century ago at Toyota. The *event* refers to a period of intense team activity aimed at dramatically improving an area or process. The RIE has become a popular method that is used in a wide variety of contexts.

The steps for a typical RIE are

1. Identify a process that needs radical improvement.

2. Assign an executive champion as the RIE's sponsor who sets the ground rules and has the clout to remove roadblocks and get proposed improvements approved.

3. Put together a team of empowered and improvement-oriented people from all affected areas and assign it an experienced facilitator. When it will help, the team can include a few outside stakeholders, such as vendors, customers, or ordinary citizens.

4. Train the team in the CI concepts/tools it will need to attack the problem.

5. Complete any necessary preparation before the event, such as gathering data, information, and resources that the team will need.

6. Give all team members a few days of release time for the event—usually one to five days, depending upon the nature of the area or process being improved.

7. Hold the event, with a strong bias for immediate action to implement changes as part of it. The early kaizen events emphasized a "ready, fire, aim" ethos in order to get the teams to make changes at a fast pace. The later-generation RIEs we studied in the public sector tended to take a more measured approach, making certain that all stakeholders were on board before implementing changes, and making doubly certain that they were not violating any rules or legal requirements.

8. At the end of the event, document all the changes as well as any new procedures. Make a to-do list of the improvements that could not be immediately implemented. Divide these medium- and long-term tasks among the team.

9. Post event, conduct regular follow-through on unfinished tasks until they are completed. Provide any necessary training

in the new procedures, and for a period of time, monitor the changes that were made to ensure they are still in place and delivering their promised results.

A good example of an RIE took place in the City of Denton, Texas, which has a population of 130,000 and 3,000 city employees. The city hired Harry Kenworthy, a former executive at the Rogers Corporation and one of the pioneers of RIEs in government, to lead Denton through its first event. Kenworthy began by asking the city's leadership team to identify a process that could use substantial improvement. They selected the city's hiring process because it affected every department and was notoriously slow and labor intensive. The project was also a low-risk first RIE for the city because hiring was largely an internal process that did not directly affect external stakeholders.

At the time, the hiring process was taking more than sixty-five days on average. It was frustrating, time-consuming, and rife with errors. Several members of the team referred to it as a "gauntlet"—managers had to spend an inordinate amount of time justifying and processing each hire.

Earlier, Kenworthy had been hired to teach a three-day workshop on CI to a select group of managers and employees from across the city. The RIE team included four people who had attended that workshop, each representing a different department that did a lot of hiring. The team also included two people from Human Resources (HR), who were the subject-matter experts, and two neutral individuals who had no direct stake in the outcome of the event. The role of the neutral participants was to add fresh perspectives by asking questions that people too close to the hiring process might overlook. This promoted higher-quality thinking by forcing team members to consider every step more carefully and to not overlook any potential improvements because of their familiarity with the hiring process.

The team began the RIE by mapping out the current hiring process. It then went through the process step by step to determine which steps were value-adding, which were non–value-adding and could be eliminated, and which could be streamlined. Before eliminating or modifying any steps, the team analyzed a considerable amount of data provided by the HR department.

It was quickly determined that many of the problems with the hiring process stemmed from years earlier when the city had to impose a two-year hiring freeze during the Great Recession (2007 to 2009). During that freeze, a lot of hurdles had been put in place to ensure that only the most critical positions were filled. However, after the freeze was lifted, these hurdles had remained embedded in the process. One, for example, required every position to be approved by an assistant city manager. Once this person approved the position, it then had to go to the city manager for final approval. Unfortunately, the meeting required for this last approval took place only once every two weeks.

Another realization was that the application window for positions was often left open for more than a month, but 25 percent of jobs were filled by people who applied in the first twenty-four hours, and 70 percent by people who applied within the first week. The window could be shortened to seven days, or fourteen days at the longest, with no appreciable negative consequences.

Because the RIE is intensive and quick, it can miss important things, which can cause the situation to revert to what it was before. The key to avoiding this lies in the preparation for the event and the follow-through afterward.

The process required all applications to go directly to HR, which checked to see if the applicant met the minimum qualifications for the job. HR's practice had been to hold all the applications until the application period closed and then dump them all at once on the hiring departments. Only then could managers begin reviewing and processing the candidates. The purpose of this policy was to keep managers from starting interviews and making job offers while the application period was still open. But with a tighter application window and a clear explanation of protocols, the process was changed to allow managers access to individual applications as soon as HR had vetted them.

Managers were also getting too many applications—an average of sixty-four per open position. Reviewing them all took considerable time. The RIE team discovered that the job application software the city used could incorporate additional questions to probe for specific experience and skills. Once managers were informed of this option, they began to incorporate screening questions in each job's application form. This helped them to quickly identify the candidates who merited closer attention, which saved time and sped up their screening.

The hiring process included many smaller non–value-adding steps. For example, the HR department had to check each hiring request to ensure it had been completed correctly. There were several common errors—one, for instance, was that the hiring department would fail to include its account number. Without this number it was difficult for HR to determine where the position was located, whether it was a vacancy or new hire, and that it wasn't a double hire. The team performed a comprehensive analysis of past errors and omissions, then clarified the form and put in countermeasures to prevent all the common mistakes. In addition, the team created several checklists to help avoid omissions and had HR insert several hiring topics into the training program for new supervisors.

Some non–value-adding steps could be eliminated with IT solutions. For example, because several assistant city managers preferred not to use the online job application system, HR had to create a pdf version of its forms that could be printed off, filled out, taken to a copier to be scanned, and then emailed back to HR for manual entry into the system. When the process analysis revealed this non–value-adding work, it was agreed that the recalcitrant assistant managers would receive coaching and help, but from now on, they would be required to use the online system like everyone else.

When requesting a new position, the old hiring process required managers to create a full hiring requisition package—which even mandated a cover memo that justified the department's existence—before the new position would be considered. Now, the position must be approved *before* the requisition is created, and the cover memo is no longer required, saving managers a lot of time, particularly if the position is denied.

Another improvement helped managers be considerably more efficient at the interview stage. Before, managers would invite as many as ten people in for interviews, just to make sure good candidates were not missed. Now, managers are encouraged to start with short phone interviews comprising a limited set of screening questions to quickly narrow the field. Only the strongest three or four candidates are then invited for in-person interviews.

In total, the team eliminated ten non–value-adding steps from the hiring process, cut twenty-five days out of it, and saved (conservatively) 688 hours of staff time annually.

The Denton RIE was large and complex. The implementation of all the resulting improvements continued for six months after the event. It had citywide impact, however, as the hiring process touched every one of the city's departments, managers, and supervisors.

The RIE is a versatile tool that can be used in a variety of contexts and on a variety of problems. For example, as discussed in Chapter 1, the Colorado Department of Health Care Policy and Financing uses four-hour RIEs to address less-complex issues. The appropriate people are brought together with the goal of developing improvements that can be implemented immediately following the meeting.

There is one caveat on the use of RIEs. Because they are intensive and quick, they can miss important things, which can cause the situation to revert to what it was before the event. This can happen for a number of reasons:

- The team misses a critical piece of information, so the old way is actually still better.

- The team fails to dig out and eliminate the root causes of some problems and designs the new process around the assumption that these problems have been eliminated when, in fact, they haven't been.

- Time is not taken to document and communicate the new procedures to everyone who needs to know about them, so the team's proposed changes are never actually implemented.

- Once the team disperses at the end of the event, the list of remaining action items is not followed through on, leaving much of the old process in place. Worse, the incomplete transformation of the process can mean the new process is inferior to the old one.

- There is not enough post-event follow-through and support to ensure that people use the improved methods long enough to develop them as new work routines.

Make certain to have people on the team who use the process being targeted by the RIE. They are in the best positions to ensure that the improvement actions cover everything, and they have the biggest stake in making the new process work.

The key to avoiding these issues lies in the pre- and post-phases of the RIE. First, make certain to include people who use the process in the RIE. They have the biggest stake in making the event a success and are in the best positions to ensure that the improvement actions cover everything. They will make certain the solutions are used. Second, choose an effective and experienced facilitator who can ensure both the quality of the group's thinking and that it does not take shortcuts. Third, don't skip Step 9—the follow-up. Once the intense RIE period is over, it is easy for team members to slip back into their regular routines and forget about their follow-up assignments. Do not consider an RIE finished until all the follow-up items are completed, everyone is trained on the new process, and several checks are made over a period of weeks or months to make sure the new processes are being followed and working well.

The A3 Process

The A3, another widely-used approach created at Toyota, is less prone to many of the problems with RIEs, mainly because it is usually used at a more measured pace. A3 refers to the international paper size—approximately 11.7 by 16.5 inches—that the problem-solving template fits onto. This template ensures that users follow the essential elements of structured problem-solving and keep their thinking focused enough to fit on a single sheet.

Although there are a number of minor variations in the A3 processes that different organizations use, they all follow the same general method. A typical template—like the one used by Results Washington in Figure 9.1 for example—incorporates the following seven steps:

1. Background—Identify the problem being addressed and why.

2. Current Condition—Spell out the problem using data if possible.

3. Goal—Set specific targets.

4. Analysis—Using appropriate CI analytical tools, identify the root causes of the problem.

5. Proposal—List proposed countermeasures that will be implemented and the desired future state.

6. Plan—Lay out who will do what, by when, and how they will do it.

7. Follow up—What are any remaining issues and actions to take?

The A3 process is robust and versatile and can be used to help solve a vast range of problems. The simplest applications of this method that we encountered dealt with modest-size problems where a bit of structured thinking was useful. The UK's Royal Mint uses A3s in this manner (see Chapter 11). The most complex situation where we saw the method applied was to Washington State's effort to get a breakthrough on a very difficult politically charged problem involving its oyster industry. We tell this story in the next chapter, where we also discuss more about the A3.

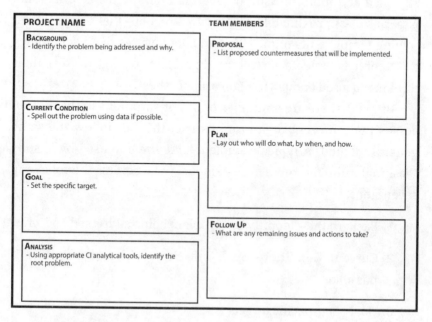

Figure 9.1: A Typical A3 Template

Many resources are available for learning more about RIEs and A3 problem-solving. The classic book on the A3 process is *Managing to Learn* by John Shook.[2] There are also many excellent videos available on the internet that explain these processes and demonstrate their use.

10

Solving High-Level Complex Problems

Most high-level complex problems are *systems*-level problems. They cut across multiple processes, and they are rarely solved with a single "home-run" solution. They consist of interconnected sub-problems, each having its own contributing factors that must be identified and addressed. Solving such problems is like running a campaign. It requires strong organizational skills, considerable resources, and a concerted effort over a long period of time. Along the way, the campaign will need to call on a variety of CI methods—including those in the last two chapters—in order to analyze and solve various elements of the larger problem. And there is always the danger that the complexity and scale of the problem make the effort vulnerable to being hijacked by political actors with high stakes in the outcome. Without solid systems thinking, and a well-planned and fact-based problem-solving strategy, a great deal of time and money can be wasted without much headway being made.

In this chapter, we discuss the three high-level methods that we found in most frequent use in the front-line–driven CI initiatives we studied: Six Sigma, the A3 (extending our treatment in the last chapter), and value-stream mapping. Each is designed to help make sense out of complex problems, to keep the team from taking shortcuts on its way to finding the root causes of the problem, and to make sure these causes are addressed effectively.

Six Sigma

Although the general method has a long history, the term *Six Sigma* emerged at Motorola in the 1980s and was made famous by Jack Welch, CEO of GE, when he strongly championed its use throughout his company and very publicly extolled its merits. In Six Sigma, the problem-solving teams follow the *DMAIC* sequence. DMAIC is an acronym for *define* the problem; put in place *measures* that can be used to drive and track improvement; gather data to *analyze* the problem; *improve* the situation; and then put in place *controls* to sustain the improvement. The formal Six Sigma process usually involves the team being led or advised by an experienced problem-solver with green-belt or black-belt certification. Such certifications are earned through a combination of training and performance on actual projects.

> Most high-level complex problems are systems-level problems, and solving them is like running a campaign. It requires strong organizational skills, considerable resources, and a concerted effort over a long period of time.

We came across a good example of a front-line–driven Six Sigma project at the Soleil Levant (Rising Sun) school, a public K–8 school in the Francophone South district of the province of New Brunswick. New Brunswick is the only officially bilingual province in Canada, and it has separate French and English school systems. Francophone South was the first district selected by the Minister of Education to implement Lean Six Sigma.

Ironically, Monique Boudreau, the district superintendent, had never wanted to be an administrator. Her interest was in helping students with special needs. But she had experienced years of frustration seeing her work have little impact. Often, she would develop learning plans with teachers for their special-needs students, only to watch those teachers encounter too many obstacles and be unable to implement the plans. When she was strongly encouraged to apply for the superintendent position by her colleagues, she thought that maybe it would enable her to make some important changes. So she applied and soon found herself the superintendent of a district with thirty-six schools.

Boudreau had little administrative experience but was the veteran of many "education reforms" that all seemed to have great potential but never delivered on their promise. Shortly after being appointed, she was asked by the province's Office of Strategy Management to take a five-day course on Lean Six Sigma (i.e., Six Sigma inflected with lean concepts) for leaders. Her staff told us that when she returned from the training, she was so excited that they thought she had gone crazy. She explained that she had finally found what she had been missing all these years—a system of management that focused on enabling the teachers and local administrators to identify and solve the problems they faced. She then sent her entire staff off for green-belt training. Two of them continued on to get black belts. Boudreau then put out an invitation to all the district's school principals, asking who would be willing to pilot Lean Six Sigma in their schools. Seven principals expressed an interest. Soleil Levant was one of three schools that Boudreau chose for the first wave.

In February 2016, Monique Vautour, the principal of Soleil Levant, began a three-month-long green-belt course. Classroom training typically took place one day a week, and between classes the participants were required to work on their individual green-belt projects. For her project, Vautour chose to work on the low literacy rate of her school's fourth grade students. The percentage of children reading at the age-appropriate level was a shockingly low 22 percent.

Vautour put together a team of eight people, including her vice principal and her third, fourth, and fifth grade teachers. The team's mission was to dig out the causes of the low literacy rate and fix as many of them as possible. Over the next three months, the team used various Lean Six Sigma techniques to identify 156 opportunities for improvement (OFIs).

Returning from her Lean Six Sigma training, the district superintendent said that she had finally found what she had been missing all these years— a system of management that focused on enabling the teachers and local administrators to identify and solve the problems they faced.

According to Vautour, the team's most important realization from its analysis was that "We were the problem, not the children." One major problem was that there was no standard way of teaching. Although learning specialists at district headquarters had developed a twenty-five-step teaching process, they also had encouraged teachers to use only the parts they felt were most relevant. Unfortunately, this led to inconsistent delivery with different teachers teaching different things using different approaches. When changing grades, the students had to adjust to an entirely new style of teaching, which made learning difficult. To fix this problem, the team developed a simplified standard procedure to teach reading. The original two-hour twenty-five-step process was streamlined down to twenty-five minutes and five steps, and it was focused on what the team thought would work best for the students. And because the teachers themselves were involved in developing this process, they felt empowered to propose modifications to the procedure if something wasn't working in their classrooms.

Many of the problems the team identified involved missing materials, wasted time, and distractions in the classroom. Some of them were easy to fix, while others took more creativity and effort:

- During intensive reading periods, there were frequent interruptions. Other teachers or staff would come into a classroom looking for something or wanting to ask the teacher a question. The public-address system was constantly paging someone or making a general announcement. Now teachers hang Do Not Disturb signs on the door during intensive reading periods, and the public-address system is no longer used during class time.

- While reading, many children were easily distracted by noise. The team purchased noise-cancelling headsets for students to wear during their reading time.

- Teachers were spending a great deal of time hunting down missing or lost reading materials. A special room was set aside for storing shared reading material, and a two-week-long project was undertaken to label, sort, and organize it. A sign-out procedure was created to assure that it would be instantly clear who had which materials and when they would be returned.

- When assistant teachers called in sick, which happened regularly, their temporary substitutes often did not know how their assigned teachers ran their classrooms, and what the assistants' roles were. The project team worked with all the teachers to document their approach to teaching and what they expected from their assistants.

- To ensure the effectiveness of the questions used to test comprehension of newly adopted reading material, a new procedure was put in place to have other teachers validate the questions before they were assigned.

■ Poor testing conditions were making it difficult for students to concentrate during the all-important annual province-wide exam. To improve the situation, two weeks before the test the teachers started monitoring the students in order to identify anything that might distract them during the exam. Teachers also spent considerable time talking with the students about appropriate behavior during the test and took steps to ensure each student was comfortable, quiet, and had a well-delineated workspace during the test. On test day, all teachers were on deck to make certain there were no disruptions.

■ The province-wide reading exam comprised three exercises and lasted 1.5 hours. Unfortunately, many of the students were only completing one or two of these exercises because they could not concentrate for the full time period. The team developed an exercise to help the students increase the length of time they could concentrate. The teachers first explained to the students the importance of being able to concentrate and how they were going to work on building their concentration skills. Once a week, the teachers put large timers in front of the class and set a goal for the students to concentrate. During this time, no one could go to the bathroom, no one could approach the teacher with a question, and no one could leave their desk. When most of the students had reached this time goal, it would be increased by five minutes the following week. As a result, a significantly higher number of students completed the full exam.

The Lean Six Sigma team started working through its OFIs in February, prioritizing them according to their potential impact and ease of implementation. By September, 59 percent of the students were scoring at the appropriate literacy level, and the project went into the control phase.

The control phase of the Six Sigma project involved the daily management of the new teaching process using a PDCA (plan-do-check-act) board.[1] Initially, the team met around this board every day after classes to review student performance on that day's reading exercises, to discuss how well recently implemented improvements had worked out, to identify new problems that had arisen, and to brainstorm further improvements. Over time, the group was able to reduce the frequency of these meetings to several times a week.

During the meeting, the teachers reviewed problems using a Pareto chart on the PDCA board.[2] The problem categories listed on the chart were identified from answers to the question, "What stopped me from following the five stages of my daily procedure for teaching reading?" The Pareto chart helped the team pick the most prevalent problems to solve first. On one of our visits to the school, five problems had been written on the board: "Interruption by an adult" (which had occurred eight times); "Public-address announcement calling a student" (six times); "Lack of cooperation from a student" (four times); "Technology not functioning well" (three times); and "A thunderclap distracted the children" (1 time). In the next daily management meeting, the team discussed these issues and decided what to do about them. Right next to the Pareto chart were two other areas of the board that dealt with actions needed: one for improvement ideas, and one for urgent actions. A final area of the board was titled Our Successes, where the group recorded its "wins" as it continued to make improvements.

An interesting tactic the teachers used was to extend the Pareto chart directly into their classrooms and have the students themselves identify and post the problems that they faced in the reading exercises and then help brainstorm solutions to them.

A year and a half into the project, the student cohort that took the province-wide exams was at a 61 percent literacy rate, a statistic that included a number of special needs students who were unable to even take the test. Without counting these students, the literacy rate would have been 78 percent—quite an improvement from 22 percent!

More on the A3 Process

In the last chapter, we discussed the A3 as an approach to mid-level problem-solving, but it is equally useful for higher-level issues.

Although Six Sigma and A3 follow essentially the same steps, they come from very different traditions. Six Sigma has its roots in engineering and quality management and puts a heavy emphasis on statistics and process control. It was developed to reduce the manufacturing defect rate of Motorola's communications equipment to less than 3.4 defects per million opportunities. Just like lean, Six Sigma has since migrated out of manufacturing and become a commonplace CI method.

The A3 was developed at Toyota as a general problem-solving method. While it is every bit as rigorous as Six Sigma, it puts a premium on communication and consensus building. When applied to large complex problems, the considerable dialogue that typically takes place during the creation of the A3 document ensures that the perspectives and insights of all key stakeholders are included, which leads to much more robust and sustainable solutions. The emphasis on communication and consensus also makes the A3 a good framework for dealing with complicated and politically charged issues. We tracked an A3 used in this way when a Results Washington team took on the largest, most complex, and most politically charged issue we encountered during our research—solving a big problem for the state's oyster industry.[3]

Although Six Sigma and A3 follow essentially the same steps, they come from different traditions. Six Sigma has its roots in engineering and quality management and puts a heavy emphasis on statistics and process control. While the A3 is every bit as rigorous as Six Sigma, it puts a premium on communication and consensus building.

The problem was that heavy rainfalls flushed a lot of contaminants into the Puget Sound, and the resulting high fecal coliform levels forced the closure of thousands of acres of oyster beds along the coast. The closures lasted until the levels of fecal coliform returned to normal. These closures disrupted the oyster supply chain, which was an important and highly visible sector of the state's economy. The state decided to try to solve the problem in one area—Samish Bay, about eighty miles north of Seattle—and then apply what was learned there to the other oyster-farming areas.

The Clean Samish Initiative (CSI), a coalition of local and state stakeholders, was the primary local group working on the problem. Early on the CSI made excellent headway, finding and eliminating the major sources of contaminants. But after two years, progress had plateaued, with fecal coliform levels still too high to avoid frequent shellfish bed closures. The difficulty was that the remaining sources of contamination were highly decentralized and hard to pinpoint and correct. Furthermore, key stakeholders were blaming each other for the problem. The shellfish farmers blamed the dairy farmers; the dairy farmers blamed homeowners with faulty septic systems; and some people blamed dogs, beavers, and even geese. Complicating the picture further was the fact that different parts of the problem fell under the jurisdiction of twenty-four different local, state, and federal authorities and four Native American tribes.

To break out of this impasse, the governor turned to Results Washington. Stew Henderson, the Results Washington facilitator assigned to the project, began the initiative by creating a draft A3 and circulating it among the various stakeholders. Their comments were incorporated into a revised draft, which was again shared with the various stakeholders. This process was repeated many times, gradually forging a consensus about what the problem was, and the best way to attack it. One shared understanding that emerged from this exercise was that the remaining sources of fecal coliform were small, highly idiosyncratic, and more numerous and disaggregated than those previously addressed. Because of this, according to the final A3, the best people to root out and eliminate these sources were the local experts on the front lines "working together and with free reign to test innovative out-of-the-box solutions."

With consensus achieved on the path forward, Henderson set up a three-day summit for representatives of key stakeholder groups, with the goal of developing a ninety-day action plan. The ground rules for the summit were

> *No stone will be left unturned. All potential causes of the fecal coliform problem will be thoroughly examined, wherever this takes us. We will use a fact-driven approach, which will require a better data-gathering strategy.*[4]

The group used many different CI tools over the three days and came up with a comprehensive action plan.

Over the next year, volunteers trudged the streams and creeks in the Samish River watershed to pinpoint sources of fecal coliform, inspectors fanned out to clean up septic systems, and agricultural inspectors helped farmers implement best practices in fencing and runoff mitigation. Local authorities ran TV advertising campaigns and local schools taught children about the problem. Surprising even the participants, during the second year of the campaign, there was only *one* shellfish bed closure after a heavy rainstorm, a dramatic reduction from the two previous years. The process of developing the A3 document had played a vital role in pulling the disparate stakeholders together to agree on the problem and a strategy to address it.

Value-Stream Mapping

The third technique for complex high-level problems that we encountered frequently is *value-stream mapping*. This can be thought of as an enhanced process flowcharting method in which the steps are laid out sequentially, but each step is also annotated with key performance measures. The measures to display are determined by the performance goals for the overall process, which might be speed, quality, service level, inventory, cost, environmental impact, or some other factor. The resulting diagram showing the contribution of each step to the overall performance of a complex process makes value-stream mapping a powerful tool for directing attention to where improvement efforts will have the biggest impact.

Value-stream mapping takes time, but it can be well worth the effort. Many of the higher-performing government organizations we studied had such maps displayed prominently, and the maps were updated regularly as the operations underlying the processes were improved. The visual nature of the maps kept staff aware of the changes and guided their thinking about the next round of improvements.

The most extensive value-stream map we encountered during our research was at the British Library, the national library of the United Kingdom and one of the largest libraries in the world. It is a legal deposit library, which means it must keep a copy of any publication copyrighted in the UK. It has over 170 million items to manage, which are held in a variety of forms and locations. Its reading rooms are open to the public, and for a small fee, anyone can request copies of documents or articles in storage. The value-stream map we went through laid out the library's dauntingly complex document retrieval process. It was so large that it wrapped entirely around the walls of a large room. The improvement team that created the map referred to it regularly both to maintain a high-level perspective on the process and to prioritize their improvement activities.

There are many good resources available on Six-Sigma and Lean Six Sigma. For a good explanation of value-stream mapping, we recommend Mike Rother and John Shook's book *Learning to See.*[5] For an insightful read on problem-solving in general, we recommend Ken Watanabe's classic and very-easy-to-read *Problem-Solving 101,* which was originally written to improve the problem-solving thinking of Japanese schoolchildren.[6] It became an international bestseller when their parents started reading it.

11

Pulling It All Together:
The UK Royal Mint's Full Spectrum of
Problem-Solving Approaches

Every year, since 1282, the Trial of the Pyx is held in London, where the trustworthiness of Great Britain's currency is verified. Throughout the year before each trial, the Deputy Master of the Royal Mint is required to set aside a random sample of several thousand new coins to be tested. Formerly held in the Palace of Westminster, today it is held at Goldsmiths' Hall, the headquarters of the Worshipful Company of Goldsmiths, and presided over by the Queen's Remembrancer, one of Britain's most senior judges. The results are reported to the Treasury.

The Royal Mint was founded by Alfred the Great in the ninth century. For most of its history it was located in, or adjacent to, the Tower of London. One of the key roles of government is to establish and maintain a strong and trusted currency. After Henry VIII debased the currency by mixing copper into the precious metals used for making coins, his daughter Queen Elizabeth I became personally involved in setting British coins back on a firm footing. Sir Isaac Newton, one of the more famous Masters of the Mint, was influential in raising its scientific and technical capabilities. In 1971, the Mint was relocated to Llantrisant, near Cardiff, in Wales.

The Royal Mint has always cultivated a culture of the highest craftsmanship and technical skill. And to stay a step ahead of counterfeiters, the Royal Mint has long emphasized continuous improvement in its operations and coins. A number of its current senior managers began as apprentices, and from the beginning their masters pressed upon them the importance of constantly making improvements. Now, as senior leaders, they continue to imbue their organization and its people with this fundamental philosophy.

Consistent with this improvement culture, over the years the operational leaders of the Mint have studied various new improvement methodologies as they have emerged, such as Total Quality Management (TQM), the Deming approach, and the Theory of Constraints. They have taken practices from these methodologies that they viewed as helpful, often adapting them considerably to fit the Mint's needs. This organic pattern of improvement changed dramatically in 2010, when the Mint was given the responsibility of producing the medals for the 2012 London Olympics. It was a high-profile no-fail project that needed to be done under considerable time pressure. At the time, the commemoratives division of the Mint, which was tasked to produce the medals, worked to the most exacting standards using traditional batch-and-queue methods. When Leighton John, the head of the division, and his staff calculated that in order to get the work done on schedule the Mint would need to hire 150 more workers and build three more vaults, he immediately assigned one of his managers to look for available real estate.

It was clear to John and his staff that even if the Mint was able to acquire suitable facilities and hire additional workers quickly, it would still be impossible to train the new workforce to the exacting standards needed and get the new facilities up and running in time to complete the project on schedule. The commemorative division was going to have to completely change the way it worked in order to meet its deadline.

John pulled together a group to lead the medal effort and study how to apply the concepts of lean to produce the medals more efficiently. It so happened that Cardiff University, which was located just a few miles away, was a European center for lean.[1] The Olympic medals group was able to involve one of its professors in its lean transformation effort. The group quickly realized that the commemorative metals production process was highly segmented, not just by physical walls in the old building, but in the way tasks were compartmentalized. So, their first step was to knock out a lot of walls, both physical and conceptual. Some of the physical walls proved quite difficult to demolish, as they were solid brick and more than eighteen inches thick! To attack the conceptual walls, the group set up a special stand-alone process for making the Olympic medals and worked on optimizing it using lean and a highly engaged workforce.

The Olympic medal crisis provided the leadership team with an epiphany. They realized that they could no longer count on the Mint's strong culture alone to drive improvement fast enough. They needed to formalize it into a comprehensive front-line–driven CI initiative.

In the old process, commemorative medals traveled some 7.5 kilometers around the facility while moving between operations. In the new process this distance was reduced to 122 meters. The old process was excruciatingly slow. For example, the very first step after the raw metals arrived at the Mint was to quarantine them for three days so that the quality department could verify their metallurgical specifications. The actual checks took only four minutes! After a lot of process changes, productivity skyrocketed and instead of having to buy new real estate, some 25 percent of the department's space was freed up. Five mezzanines (half floors) that had been built to create more workspace were taken out. Through its lean transformation, the commemorative division was able to meet its Olympic obligations without a hitch.

The same process being adopted for the Olympic medals project was also applied to the rest of the commemoratives division, with impressive results. The newly increased speed of coins moving through production allowed work-in-process inventory to be reduced from 3,500 tons to 750—a drop of almost *80 percent*.

The Olympic medal crisis provided the leadership team with an epiphany. Although they had always believed in CI, they realized that they could no longer count on the Mint's strong culture to drive improvement fast enough. They needed to formalize the Mint's CI program, starting with what had been learned in the commemoratives division. And because most of the senior leaders had begun their careers at the Mint as apprentices, they knew that their new initiative should be front-line driven.

A Blend of CI Tools and Techniques

The Royal Mint has developed a full spectrum of CI methods. The scope and range of this spectrum is illustrated in the following parts.

Front-Line Level Systems

Daily management of problems is done through the Mint's tier board process, which is similar to Arizona's huddle-board system described in Chapter 8. At 8:30 each morning, every front-line team meets for fifteen minutes or so around its Tier 1 board to discuss any issues that arose the previous day, how to deal with them, and what can be expected that day. Any problems that the teams need higher-level support to solve are escalated to their Tier 2 board, where their team leaders and middle managers, as well as representatives from each support function, meet at 10:30. If the Tier 2 meeting cannot resolve or handle an issue, it is escalated to the Tier 3 board for senior leadership. Twice a week, the leadership team—including Anne Jessopp, the CEO—meets around this board to address the issues on it and to agree upon the actions to take. All three tiers of boards are public and are organized around the Mint's five focus areas: safety, people, quality, delivery, and finance (SPQDF).

The Small Improvement Opportunity (SIO) system promotes and documents improvement ideas from front-line workers. Whenever front-line employees see opportunities for improvement that they can do themselves (or with the permission of their supervisor), they write out—either online or on a special form—a short description of the problem and how they solved it. Currently, every front-line employee is expected to complete at least one SIO per month.

Top leaders play direct and visible roles in recognizing front-line engagement and improvement activity. One manager commented to us that this direct involvement by senior leaders has a much greater impact than the rewards scheme.

As part of the Cheers Cheques program, to promote and recognize front-line engagement, managers and team leaders give small rewards to staff as thank-yous for a job well done. There are a variety of rewards available, from gift cards and cinema vouchers to bottles of wine. The largest reward is a £50 ($65) gift card for a nice local restaurant.

Top leaders play direct and visible roles in recognizing front-line engagement and improvement activity. Whenever a front-line team has a success, such as getting good feedback from a government authority or making a significant improvement, the CEO or COO visits that team to share the good news and learn more about the improvement. One manager commented to us that this direct involvement by senior leaders has a much greater impact than the rewards scheme. It makes the staff proud and reminds them of how critical their work is for the Royal Mint's mission.

Mid-Level and Complex Problems

When solving problems that require more extensive analysis, the method of choice is the A3, discussed in the last two chapters. In 2014, all managers and supervisors at the Mint were trained in A3 problem-solving, and today each is expected to complete at least two A3 improvement projects per month. Although front-line workers have not been specifically trained in A3s, they work with the method extensively as team members on improvement projects led by managers or support staff.

A clever rapid reaction system created by the Mint is the *Balloon-Up* process. If a potentially significant problem arises that needs immediate action, any manager can call a Balloon-Up meeting. All the relevant experts and managers drop whatever they are doing and convene to discuss the problem. Typically, they determine a temporary quick-fix as well as launch a project to address the root causes of the problem—which often uses an A3 analysis. Although Balloon-Up meetings usually last thirty minutes or less, they disrupt the work of a lot of busy people. However, they actually save a great deal of time and headaches because the emergency problems are addressed quickly and before they can cause further complications. Although these meetings were used a lot when the Mint was beginning its lean transformation, today they are infrequent.

A creatively simple technique, the *Q-table*, is used for responding to defects in coins and coin-blanks. (The "Q" stands for quality.) There are five Q-tables on the Llantrisant campus set out at strategic points in the coin-making process. Any time two or more instances of a particular defect are discovered, they are bagged and left on the appropriate Q-table. Each morning managers and supervisors visit the Q-tables that are downstream from the processes they are responsible for. If the defects on a table are caused by their area, they determine what corrective action to take. When correcting a problem requires more than a quick fix, often an A3 analysis is triggered.

Focusing Capital Improvements for Maximum Impact

To ensure the Mint is getting the best use from the time, money, and energy invested in major improvement projects and upgrades, the leadership team created a highly structured prioritization system for large expenditures. It maintains a list of capital projects, including projected infrastructure maintenance and upgrades, anticipated equipment replacements based on lifecycle projections, and potential new equipment purchases. The possible expenditures are prioritized using the Theory of Constraints.

The idea behind the Theory of Constraints is that any organization's output capacity is limited by just a few bottlenecks, or constraints. No matter how much capacity is added elsewhere, overall output will not increase unless the performance of these constraints is improved. During our time at the Mint, it had just one constraint: the plating process. Most coins are plated with different metals for appearance, durability, and security. As we heard quite a few times during our time there, "An hour lost at the constraint is an hour lost forever."[2]

> The Royal Mint's capability to continuously improve has made it the gold standard in the industry. It makes coins for sixty-seven different countries and recently released the new one-pound coin, with technology that makes it one of the hardest coins in the world to counterfeit.

In 2014, the wastewater treatment plant was identified as the most critical process that needed improving. The plant's primary role was to treat the wastewater from the plating process. A CI specialist,

Jennifer Honey, was assigned to the plant to oversee its improvement process. At that time, the Mint had a full order book, and whenever the treatment plant went down, it had to either shut or slow down its plating operation with significant loss in output. It was obvious to everyone that the treatment plant was the Mint's major constraint and top priority for improvement.

Honey's goal was to set up the CI infrastructure and build a bottom-driven improvement culture and mindset within the treatment plant. To keep the plant up and running, its management and operators had become masters of firefighting and the quick fix. She had to work hard to convince them of the value of permanent fixes, stability, and predictability, which she did with great success.

Over the next few years, the group identified and fixed many problems. One of the first issues the group identified was that although the operators had a set sequence of steps to follow when processing the effluents, they did not fully understand the chemistry behind these steps. Consequently, when the process drifted, they had trouble making the right corrections to get it back under control. So the plant manager, an experienced chemist, put together a series of structured training programs, one for each step in the process.

Another big problem arose from the large variance in the type of wastewater arriving for treatment. Depending upon what was being processed by the plating department, the proper treatments could vary considerably. A major project was launched to reconfigure the pipework to provide greater flexibility in processing. And a procedure was also put in place to let the workers know the chemistry of the wastewater coming to the plant ahead of time so they could direct it into the proper tanks. Strong acids can be sent to one tank, weak acids to another, strong alkali to a third, and so on. With these changes, the operators can now easily mix the output of the holding tanks to get the most straightforward blend to process quickly and economically.

In addition to the capital improvement project, Honey estimated that while she was working with the treatment plant, the supervisors and managers there produced around forty A3s, and the staff came up with more than one hundred SIOs.

All this improvement effort paid off. By 2018, there were no lost plating hours due to the wastewater treatment plant, and the cost of running the plant had been reduced by 30 percent.

Competition among national mints is intense. But the Royal Mint's strong tradition and improvement capability has made it the gold standard in the industry and a clear leader in both quality and efficiency. It produces more than 5 billion coins a year and makes coins for sixty-seven different countries.

In 2017, the Royal Mint released the new one-pound coin, which has some innovative security features that make it one of the hardest coins in the world to counterfeit. According to Leighton John, "The new coin was right at the edge of our capability."

The Royal Mint has one of the most effective CI initiatives we have seen anywhere.

PART 4

When Government Leads the Way: Pushing the Boundaries of Innovation and Improvement

Public-sector organizations have benefitted from years of private-sector experience and learning about CI. When starting its initiative, Washington State got help from experts at some of the state's leading companies, including Starbucks and Boeing. The province of New Brunswick's effort drew on Jane Washburn's background in Lean Six Sigma from her experience working for the Irving Group, the province's largest private-sector employer. And Arizona hired consultants with prior work experience at Toyota. In Part 4 we reverse this pattern by looking at innovative improvement methods developed by four public-sector organizations—innovations that the business world could learn a great deal from.

The cases illustrate innovative ways in which leaders pulled front-line perspectives into the management decision-making enclave. These brought fresh insights and ideas into higher-level decisions that made them more responsive to the actual situations involved and led to far better outcomes.

In Chapter 12, we examine how The Regional Municipality of York in Ontario, Canada, deployed three novel techniques to increase employee engagement and get ideas from large numbers of front-line employees on important issues that are traditionally the exclusive domain of management. Chapter 13 looks at how the UK's Highways England closed a large budget gap by using its purchasing power to meld its suppliers (many of whom were direct competitors) into a single giant learning machine. It set up a process by which front-line leaders shared improvement ideas with each other—vertically, horizontally, and across organizational boundaries. In Chapter 14, we examine how Denver, Colorado, the first major city to legalize recreational marijuana, established an innovative front-line–based process to quickly spot emerging issues in the rapidly evolving cannabis market. Denver's ability to respond to emerging issues before they became big problems was much of the reason it has become a global benchmark for the regulation of legalized marijuana. Lastly, Chapter 15 tells the story of Denmark's MindLab, the world's original policy innovation laboratory. By using design thinking and a continuous improvement loop that put policymakers on the front lines to observe the effects of their policies, it created a new model for how any large organization can develop policies that are significantly more effective.

These four organizations are examples of where the public sector is clearly pushing the boundaries of CI.

12

York Region's Innovative Engagement Methods

The Regional Municipality of York in Ontario, Canada, has used several novel approaches to get its employees engaged in improvement activity. Located just north of Toronto, York Region includes nine municipalities, and has a rapidly growing population of over 1.2 million. Its government employs a highly diverse workforce of about five thousand and oversees a budget of some CAD$3.2 billion. In both 2019 and 2020, the region was selected as one of Canada's Best Diversity Employers, and in 2021 it was named one of the Best Places to Work for New Graduates in Canada.

One of the guiding principles of York's "Vision 2051" calls for the regional government to be innovative and creative, defined as having the "ability to transcend traditional ideas or solutions and to create meaningful new ideas or more effective solutions, processes and opportunities."[1] The region's small Office of Continuous Improvement, consisting of two people on staggered two-year assignments (on loan from their regular departments), played a pivotal role in fostering this innovation and creativity throughout the organization. In late 2014, Ted Burley, then in charge of the CI office, set up a steering committee consisting of both office staffers and two managers from each of the region's six departments. The committee decided that the highest CI priority was to get broad front-line engagement. To do this, it launched three major initiatives.

The first two, the York Den and crowdsourcing initiatives, were designed to spark large scale engagement and ideas from employees across the region. The third, the Innovation Laboratory or ILab process, is used when managers want to get input and ideas from a large group of front-line staff on a specific problem or issue.

The York Den

The York Den was marketed to employees with the tag line, "Get involved, have a say, make a difference." The concept had already been successfully piloted by the city of Guelph, Ontario. It was modeled after the British reality television show *The Dragon's Den*, which is similar to the show *Shark Tank* in the United States and *The Tigers of Money* in Japan. In York Den, employees pitched their idea to a panel of judges that comprised six front-line people, one from each of the region's major departments.

On April 1, 2016, all employees received an email inviting them to participate in York Den. If they had an idea that would improve the regional government in any way, they were asked to fill out a brief online form and describe their idea in twenty-five words or less. None of the applications were rejected, and applicants were offered the opportunity to work on their pitches with a mentor, usually a steering committee member. The program was for front-line staff only. Managers were not allowed to submit ideas.

Over a four-day period in June 2016, twenty-eight pitches were made. Each person or team submitting an idea had five to seven minutes to pitch it to the panel of judges, after which the judges could ask questions before coming to a decision.

The Chief Administrative Officer (CAO) of the region, Bruce Macgregor, had committed beforehand that the judging panel would have the authority to approve and fund any or all of the ideas. The panel approved seventeen of the ideas, forwarded three to senior management because it felt they were beyond the initial scope or budget parameters, and did not approve eight of the ideas. A week later, the judges had a four-hour meeting with the CAO, who expressed his support for every one of their decisions.

The region created a special celebration for York Den and the resulting ideas. A poster was made for each of the twenty-eight original ideas, with a summary of the pitch, the people involved in it, and what had been done with their idea. For several months, these posters lined the lobby walls of the large York Region Administrative Centre in Newmarket, Ontario. On July 7 (note the fast timeline), a barbeque celebration was held to announce which ideas had been approved and to recognize the participants and panel of judges. The chairman of York Region and the senior management team attended, along with over three hundred people. The celebration was open to all employees and attendance was strong. All the ideas were celebrated. Even people who pitched the eight ideas that had not been approved earned icare points as a thank you—*icare* is the region's recognition system in which points earned can be redeemed for various prizes. The judges had also decided on four awards for Best Ideas. The only rule was that the winning ideas had to link to one of the four priorities in the region's strategic plan, which were

1. Economic vitality

2. Healthy communities

3. Sustainable environment

4. Good governance

One of the aims of the York Den was to raise employee awareness of the region's strategic initiatives, so each team had been asked to try to frame its pitch in terms of one or more of these priorities.

The steering committee made sure that the people who had made unsuccessful pitches were not forgotten after the celebration. It arranged another opportunity for them to make their pitches, this time directly to managers in the departments their ideas would impact. Several of these ideas were adopted and implemented. As a member of the steering committee observed, they had, in fact, been good ideas, but their champions just couldn't articulate them well enough in the short presentation time to get the judges' endorsement.

Following are four examples of York Den ideas that were approved.

York Region Street View.   This idea was to use Google Street View technology to embed in Google Maps immersive views of the outside and inside of government buildings, as well as public parks and trails. The aim was to inform citizens about accessibility to government facilities and parks. People with mobility issues could see where and how best to enter a government facility, as well as which parks and trails would be accessible to them, and how.

The proposal was to hire Google-certified photographers to photograph the various locations inside and out and to upload and embed these views into Google Maps. Citizens could simply click on the map to find accessible entrances and visualize how to get to their destination inside the buildings. The group presenting the idea requested CAD$5,200 to pilot the process for two frequently visited locations, and the judges approved the funds.

Today, visitors can access the photos from Google Maps for dozens of public sites. In addition, by working officially with Google, the York Region's embedded information pages (which pop up when the map is clicked on) are Google verified and can now be modified directly by the region's staff so all ancillary information is correct and up to date.

Greenhouse Gas Reduction.   This idea, put forward by three employees who faced long commute times in the Toronto area traffic, was to extend the flextime policy so people could avoid the rush hour. The existing flextime policy required that everyone's workday include the core business hours between

9:30 a.m. and 3 p.m., which meant they would face rush hour traffic in at least one direction of their commute. The proposal was to conduct a pilot program involving some thirty employees who would volunteer to start outside congestion hours—between 6:30 and 7 a.m. or between 10 and 10:30 a.m. This would save these employees significant time and fuel.

With thirty people who had long commutes enrolled in the pilot project, the team calculated that by avoiding the heaviest traffic, they would reduce carbon emissions by some eight tons per year. Other benefits from expanding flextime included longer core hours for government operations, improved work-life balance, reduced stress, and employees saving about CAD$125 each per year in gasoline costs.

The plan was to pilot the new flextime hours for three months, collect data, and then present the results to management to see if a full-blown program would be merited. Employees in the program would use a geotracking app that they would start when leaving home and stop when arriving at work; it would track their route, as well as their arrival and departure times. In preparing its pitch for the idea, the team had talked with managers so it could address their concerns, such as how the program would affect service levels.

The data from the pilot showed that if 10 percent of the region's employees enrolled in the program, it would save 124 tons of carbon emissions per year, which was 16 percent of the region's five-year emission reduction goal. Several of the participants estimated that they would save up to two hours per day and CAD$500 in tolls as they would no longer have to use the expensive toll lanes when traveling with less congestion.

The team's greatest hope was that if the concept was proven for the York Region, other government organizations and private businesses would offer similar programs, and both travel times and carbon emissions across Greater Toronto could be reduced by as much as 20 percent.

Changing the Way People Apply for Social Housing.   High housing costs in the York Region mean that there is a lot of pressure on public housing. But the process for deciding who gets what housing was long, cumbersome, confusing, and costly. Applications were still paper-based and communications were handled through the mail. The cost to the region to mail out applications was over CAD$26,000 per year, and mailing out responses, acknowledgments, and reminders exceeded another CAD$32,000 per year. And this did not include the cost of preparing the mailings. The processing of the nineteen-page forms involved manually entering their information into the computer, which was time consuming and led to many errors. And because the application process was confusing to the public, in the first half of 2016 alone, over five hundred applications had been processed for people who were not even eligible for public housing. In spite of the number of applications doubling from six to twelve thousand per year, its staffing remained at just four people. In addition to processing all the applications, the staff handled about twenty calls per day that averaged fifteen minutes each. The bottom line: people were waiting for years to get housing.

The team proposed a new and streamlined process, with a number of improvements. One was to have general phone calls handled by Access York, a new corporate contact center set up to provide citizens with a "no wrong door" approach for all their government needs. Access York was just ramping up and was eager to include the housing team's calls. The center was staffed with service professionals equipped with translation services and a sophisticated customer relationship management (CRM) system.

Second, the team proposed an overhaul of the office's website, which was badly dated, difficult to navigate, and had a lot of potential for improvement. The new site provided clear eligibility requirements along with much more information on housing options, and included maps, views, nearby stores, and public transportation. It also allowed for online applications.

Third, instead of mailings, the team proposed using the region's newly installed Enterprise Notification System (ENS) which contacted people electronically, to save time and money. An additional advantage to using the ENS was that it could track whether messages were received or not.

The judges approved the proposal and the changes proved highly effective. Now, for example, Access York runs all of the intake and customer service functions, and recent data showed 80 percent of housing queries are answered completely on the first call. Only 10 percent of calls—the ones with complex queries or issues—are forwarded to the four housing department specialists, who can now focus on the work for which they are truly needed.

Creation of a Training Video Service Group. The thinking behind this idea was that if the region had a unit that could help people create training videos, it would save a lot of time and ensure that employees would have easy access to training when they need it. The region has lots of offices, pockets of specialized skill sets, and many people needing to know how to use certain systems and software. Rather than providing training individually, or setting up training sessions, it would be much more efficient to create training videos that people could watch when convenient and go back to review as needed. It could also be used for knowledge management—to capture knowledge that only certain individuals possessed in order to avoid losing it when they left their positions.

The team proposing the idea had already created a highly successful training video for the Region's eDocs document storage system. They had also established a set of guidelines for training videos: they should be clear, concise, and only transmit the key points. The process of creating such videos had to involve the region's legal, communications, and corporate learning departments.

When the CAO heard this idea he commented, "This is what the York Den was all about." The first three videos the group created were about the purchasing process: how to find the forms, how to get the request approved, and how to get fast-track approval when this was necessary. The videos explained all the terms involved and walked people through how to fill out the various forms and provide the necessary information. Before the videos, the purchasing staff were constantly having to provide half-day training sessions to small groups scattered around the region, and they spent a great deal of time on the phone walking employees through the purchasing process. Now employees can simply watch the appropriate video whenever they have a question.

The York Den was an enormous success. The widespread energy and interest the event generated achieved the steering committee's goal of boosting front-line staff engagement and demonstrated how useful front-line ideas could be. When describing the York Den pitches to us, Ted Burley and Joanne Armstrong from the Region's CI office made two observations. First, every presenter or team was genuinely grateful for the opportunity to have their idea heard. Second, they were all passionate about, and proud of, their ideas. It is important to note that everyone involved, from the steering committee to the York Den panel, was a volunteer.

York Crowdsourcing

Generally, every four years, the York Region contracts with an outside company to conduct an extensive employee survey. The results from such surveys can be tricky to handle. They create an expectation for employees that management will act on the areas identified as needing improvement. If management fails to do this, it can hurt morale. For a long time, York held employee focus groups after each survey where ideas for appropriate follow-up actions were brainstormed and discussed. For the 2015 survey, which had an impressive

80-percent response rate and generated thousands of written comments, York's leadership decided to take a more innovative approach to identify the actions to be taken.

The timing of the survey coincided with the York leadership team's endorsement of the use of crowdsourcing as a means to broaden employee engagement. They decided to see if crowdsourcing would be a good way to involve more employees in the post-survey discussions and whether it would lead to a more diverse set of ideas.

The crowdsourcing project was a collaboration between the CI office, IT Services, and the region's Corporate Services Department and involved the CI steering committee as well as people from HR. The project began by tabulating the survey results, reviewing the data, and reading the comments. From this analysis, and with input from the region's senior leadership team, twelve broad priority areas for improvement action were identified:

- Health, safety, and wellness

- Work-life balance

- Organizational communication

- Support from other departments

- Support for innovation and process improvement

- Respect in the workplace and harassment

- Managing underperforming employees

- Organizational change

- Support for diversity

- A charter for diversity and inclusion

- Increased benefits to cover mental health

- Modernized workspaces to support innovation and collaboration

In May 2016, the region launched the online crowdsourcing Ideathon portion of the process by inviting all its employees to provide
ideas to help address one or more of the twelve areas. Before the launch,
a group of moderators was trained. The moderators' role was to monitor and guide the online conversations. Their primary work turned out
to be nudging participants toward clarity if their ideas were too ambig-
uous and amalgamating similar ideas as part of the conversation.

The three-week crowdsourcing ideation process produced 248
ideas, 1,100 comments on these ideas, and 25,000 votes (the program
allowed employees to vote each idea up or down). One advantage of
the voting element was that participants received almost immediate
feedback through their colleagues' comments and votes. Management was taken completely out of the judging role.

A small group of the staff involved took the results of the crowdsourcing, culled the ideas that were not well received, and clustered
and clarified the remaining ones. The list of ideas, rank ordered by
the crowdsource voting, was then sent to about a hundred mid- to
upper-level managers across the organization, who were asked to rate
each idea on a four-point scale using the following criteria:

■ This solution will improve our workplace environment.

■ This solution will increase employee engagement.

■ This solution is feasible.

■ This solution will result in a positive return on investment.

The group discussed the managers' input and sought feedback
and help refining ideas from subject matter experts, who were often
the same people responsible for implementing the ideas. The resulting list of forty-four action items was submitted to the senior leadership team, which reviewed each idea, and approved all of them at a
meeting in November.

These action items included 1) adapt technology to help with
mobility and flexibility—e.g., more video conferencing and tele-
work (which laid the foundation for a smooth transition to working

remotely during the Covid pandemic); 2) streamline the process for booking conference rooms (which are always in high demand); 3) update physical space to facilitate more team-based work with more small conference rooms and flexible work spaces; and 4) improve outside spaces around buildings to create a more pleasant environment for employee breaks and exercise.

On one of our visits to York, three months after the leadership team's approval of the forty-four actions, twenty of them had already been completed, eighteen others were in process, and the last six were about to be launched. In fact, we found out that many of the action items had been underway prior to the leadership team's approval. The transparent process had meant that as managers saw good ideas emerge, they often took the initiative and began implementing them.

Several interesting aspects of the Ideathon process contributed greatly to its success. The first was its compressed timeframe. Considering the speed at which most initiatives work in large organizations, the process moved extremely fast. One of the managers involved explained that this speed was intentional and important. Once people got excited, it was vital to maintain that excitement through the entire process including the implementation phase. If the process had dragged, people would have lost interest and the positive impact of having their voices heard and seeing their ideas used would have been largely lost.

The second interesting aspect of the Ideathon process was its transparency. From the survey results, through the crowdsourcing ideas, to the final forty-four action items, the process was transparent. Anyone could track any idea at any stage in the process. This, combined with the very high correlation between the crowdsourced votes and the action items approved by top leadership, showed employees that their ideas were valued and treated fairly.

The third aspect of interest was how the Ideathon process created a safe space for innovation. As one of the managers involved in the process explained, "Government is inherently risk-averse, so the team wanted to design an approach that fit with this tradition, but one that also would allow some innovation to happen." This is why the initiative was set up as a pilot designed for York to learn about the benefits and drawbacks of crowdsourcing and how it might be used effectively in the future. A special limited-time contract had been negotiated with the software developer in order to allow York to try it before agreeing to a multiyear contract. During this trial window, in addition to using the software for the Ideathon, some twenty individual branches experimented with the software to run their own local crowdsourcing campaigns. Given that crowdsourcing software was relatively new, the software company also learned a great deal from watching how York used its product.

The York ILab Process

The York Den and crowdsourcing were exciting ways to get the employees' attention and engage them in making improvements. Both approaches were highly successful and generated a lot of good ideas, but they were limited and *ad hoc* events. Around the same time as these initiatives, the York Region also set up a permanent infrastructure for getting employee ideas, called ILab, short for Innovation Laboratory, and its meetings were often referred to internally as "innovation sessions" or "facilitated workshops." The ILab approach is a creative and highly versatile process for managers to get high-quality input and focused ideas from a large group of their employees. It is also relatively quick. The ILab workshops last from an hour and a half to four hours, depending on the issue being addressed, and can involve just a few people or up to several hundred. Between sixty and seventy times a year, managers from various governmental units request help from the CI office to organize and facilitate an ILab workshop. Many more smaller-scale sessions are facilitated locally without the involvement of the CI office.

York's ILab process is a modification of the five-step "i5" problem-solving process developed by Juice Inc., a consulting company based in Ontario, Canada. Central to i5 is the Innovation in a Box toolkit, which includes twenty-four tools and techniques to help a problem-solving team work through the steps of the i5 process. Table 12.1 lists these steps and some of the tools that can be used at each one. Most of the tools are relatively generic, but Juice cleverly demystified them for easy use, and it streamlined the process so that the output of a tool used at one step smoothly becomes the input for the tool used at the next step.

Table 12.1. The Juice Inc. i5 Process

STEP	TASK	SAMPLE TOOLS
Identification	Identify problems, needs, and possibilities.	Innovation Curve i5 Report
Investigation	Seek understanding from the big picture to root cause.	5 Whys Stakeholder Map Empathy Map
Ideation	Generate, strengthen, and elaborate ideas.	Brainstorming Mind Mapping Stimulus Response Value-Chain Analysis
Impact	Evaluate and prioritize ideas based on impact.	Good, Better, Best Braketology Paired Comparison Lotus Blossom
Implementation	Create, test, and deliver on a plan.	Gantt Charts Prototyping Strategic Game Plan

In November 2015, York kicked off the ILab initiative with a four-day Juice training session. The first group trained as process facilitators consisted primarily of the CI steering committee, which was made up of professional staff and managers from across the region's six departments.

The fifteen graduates began meeting once a month for two hours, in what they called a "Community of Practice." In the first hour, the participants typically shared experiences and insights they had gained from running ILab workshops, whether these were set up by the CI office, or were local workshops they had run in their home departments or branches. The second hour usually involved two members facilitating a short workshop, always dealing with a real problem. In this way, the members could experiment with the use of different tools or facilitation techniques in a safe environment and coach each other. (There are currently over a hundred trained facilitators in York's Community of Practice.)

York Region started with the full Juice Innovation in a Box package, which comprised four days of training on the i5 process and twenty-four tools. Since then, the CI office has entered into an agreement to provide its own Juice training internally, has streamlined the five-step i5 process down to the three-step ILab process, and has consolidated the training into a single day that teaches only eight of the twenty-four tools.

Juice's original i5 model was designed for a problem-solving team to take an issue from problem definition all the way through to solution implementation. York's ILab process uses only the ideation portion of the process: 1) collecting ideas, 2) prioritizing ideas, and 3) putting shape to ideas. Management is responsible for the two other steps—identifying the problems/issues and implementing solutions. The approach is designed for managers who want employees' perspectives and ideas on significant decisions, potential changes, or day-to-day operational challenges. An entire unit, with more than a hundred people, can engage with the issue to offer, prioritize, and flesh out ideas, all within a two-hour workshop. And because they have had significant input, employees are much more accepting of management's ultimate decision.

An ILab workshop organized by the CI office begins with a client, typically a department or branch manager, contacting the office with an issue for which employee input and ideas are desired. Staff from the office then meet with the client to create a problem statement and design an ILab workshop. A template is created that includes this problem statement, the date and time of the upcoming workshop, the number of facilitators needed, an estimate of the time commitment required for each facilitator, and any additional information that is important to its success. The template is then sent out to the hundred-plus members of the Community of Practice asking for volunteer facilitators. The CI office selects the event facilitators fròm those who volunteered, often pairing veteran and less-experienced facilitators, and arranges a meeting with the client. During the meeting, the manager's goals are discussed and a detailed workshop plan is created, including the tools that will be used. From this meeting a facilitators' guide is created by the CI office, and then the process is handed off to the facilitators.

The following examples illustrate the range of challenges the ILab process can address.

Excellence in Public Health Two of the four divisions of the Department of Public Health underwent an accreditation process from Excellence Canada, an independent organization that promotes better performance in Canadian organizations through training, certifications, and awards. The two divisions were given a comprehensive report detailing their strengths and opportunities for improvement.

A steering group was established to develop improvement plans for the two divisions based on the report's findings. The group identified four top priorities and presented them at an all-staff planning day, which included an ILab workshop. A total of 140 staff members participated in the workshop, which began with four "how might we" questions:

1. How might we better evaluate and monitor our partnerships?

2. How might we better develop innovation as a way of life in the divisions?

3. How might we better hear the voice of the customer?

4. How might we develop a comprehensive customer service plan?

Ideas to address these four questions were brainstormed, evaluated, and voted upon. Action items were developed for the best ideas.

The results from the workshop were used to develop the next year's improvement agendas for both divisions. The managers we talked with about the ILab emphasized that because the staff in both divisions was involved throughout the process, they readily got behind the improvement plans.

Improving Leadership Training for the Corporate Learning Team   The York Corporate Learning Team developed a training program for new supervisors and managers. York-Leads, as it was called, comprised eight days of instruction spread over a number of weeks. The last day was about how to lead innovation and improvement activity, with ILab as a critical component. When trying to identify an issue to use for a demonstration ILab workshop—one that all the students could readily engage with—the learning team had an inspiration. Why not use the exercise to evaluate the new leadership program?

Outside facilitators were brought in to conduct the workshop, and the Corporate Learning Team members left the room to make certain the participants could speak more freely. The class was divided into four groups, each of which began by brainstorming improvement opportunities and ideas. These ideas were ranked using the Good, Better, Best technique, and the top four were used in a Lotus Blossom exercise to develop specific action items to implement them.

While the first York-Leads program was rated quite highly, the ILab workshop still provided the Corporate Learning Team with a number of good ideas that were incorporated into the curriculum for the next class. Every York-Leads program now closes with an ILab workshop on how to improve the training experience.

Facilitating the Development of Key Performance Indicators (KPIs) During the Covid-19 pandemic, ILab workshops could no longer be held in person. So, when Allison Bailey, the program manager of the CI office, received a request from the Court Services Branch to facilitate a workshop to help it to develop a new set of budget-related key performance indicators (KPIs), the workshop had to be virtual. The goal was to create KPIs that more closely reflected the branch's current service offerings and departmental goals and that would align better with the region's strategic plan.

York Region's Court Services Branch is the second largest Provincial Offences court in Ontario. It serves the residents of the York Region, the nine area municipalities, the Province of Ontario, the Judiciary, and over thirty law enforcement and regulatory agencies operating within the regional municipality. It operates six trial courtrooms, two intake courtrooms, and three early-resolution meeting rooms.

The CI group had learned that virtual workshops worked best if they were kept to no more than ninety minutes and did not have more than a dozen or so online participants. Consequently, the facilitation plan called for splitting the effort into three forty-five-minute online sessions and having only ten participants, which included the branch team responsible for the collection, analysis, and reporting of data to the Office of the Budget.

The first online session was largely about defining the task—introducing the group to the principles behind the strategic-planning process, the steps this process followed, key terminology, how KPIs factor into accountability, and how KPIs are developed. An electronic poll was used to test each participant's knowledge, and any misunderstandings were clarified. This was followed by a virtual whiteboard exercise on how to develop KPIs. The participants were divided into two teams—Court Operations and Prosecution Services—each of which was given the homework assignment to apply the same methodology to their area and come up with a list of possible KPIs.

The second online session, or more accurately *sessions*, involved Bailey meeting with each team separately in an unstructured format to discuss their work and answer any questions about either the strategy process or the development of KPIs.

The teams submitted their proposed KPIs before the third session, which was designed as a workshop to finalize them. The session began with a discussion of the criteria for screening the proposed KPIs. The teams then met in virtual breakout rooms to apply the criteria to their lists. Upon completion, the groups reconvened, reported their final choices, and discussed how they would be used.

The virtual workshop resulted in each team creating three or four solidly actionable KPIs dealing with output and operating costs. While doing so, the participants also learning a great deal about York's strategic planning process.

When we were introduced to York Region's ILab process, it immediately caught our attention as something distinctive. It was a CI method designed for managers to get insights, ideas, and perspectives from large groups of employees on issues where such input has traditionally been exclusively from managers and experts. At the same time, the interactive format means the participants hear and evaluate each other's ideas. Only those ideas selected collectively by the participants as the best emerge from the process to be presented to managers. While these managers do not relinquish any authority over the final choices, because the employees had meaningful input into them, the decisions are well received, and usually better.

13

Highways England and Its Continuously Improving Supply Chain

Note: This chapter draws in part from an article we wrote for the *Journal of Government Financial Management.* We are grateful to the journal for permission to incorporate that material here.[1]

P rivate sector companies play a major role in government performance. Not only do they supply a great many goods and services, but they also perform many government functions and deliver a variety of government-sponsored services. Accordingly, outcomes—in terms of costs, quality, and service levels—are highly dependent upon the performance of these independent organizations. The challenge becomes how to get the best value from private sector providers and encourage them to continuously improve.

The traditional approach has been to create contracts with a comprehensive list of performance specifications and then award these contracts to the qualified bidder with the lowest price. Although this approach generally gets the job done, it often proves hollow, inflexible, and devoid of any real opportunities to learn and improve. How can government create supplier relationships that focus on continuously improving performance, and how can the benefits of the higher levels of value created be equitably shared? In this chapter we examine a unique example of how a public-sector organization did exactly that.

Highways England (HE), the government enterprise responsible for building and maintaining England's primary motorway system, had a problem. (Note: In August 2021, Highways England changed its name to National Highways, but we have chosen to stay with the name of the organization at the time we studied it.) The budget it had been given for the next five years was £1.2 billion[2] less than the cost of the work it was required to undertake. Two things were clear. First, with 95 percent of the agency's funds going to external contractors, there was no hope of bridging this gap by finding savings and efficiencies within HE itself. Second, simply issuing requests for proposals and choosing the lowest bids was not going to make up much of this difference. HE was already getting highly competitive prices. It needed to completely recast its approach to working with contractors in order get substantially more value for its money. So it developed an innovative approach to selecting and working with suppliers, one designed to drive dramatic performance improvement throughout its supply chain.

Background

Highways England is a 3,500-person British government enterprise whose charge is to modernize, maintain, and operate England's 4,300 miles of core motorways. Although these highways represent only 2.4 percent of England's roads, they move a third of its traffic and two-thirds of its heavy truck traffic. HE was created when a former government agency—the Highways Agency—was converted to a government-owned enterprise on April 1, 2015. This was done in order to insulate its funding from the whims of the annual government budgeting process and to give its managers increased freedom and flexibility in running the organization. The change came about as a result of the realization by UK political leaders that better roads were vital for economic growth and would greatly improve their constituents' quality of life. The new organization was given five years of funding tied to an ambitious set of goals. This included £11 billion in capital programs and £15 billion in road upgrades (installing smart highways, adding lanes, resurfacing roads, improving road drainage, etc.).

With the lion's share of the annual highways budget going to private sector contractors, the former Highways Agency had already started to concentrate improvement efforts on its supply chain. It began by strongly encouraging suppliers to adopt the principles of lean construction management to improve their process efficiency, to eliminate waste, and to complete work more quickly. Although a few cutting-edge companies have successfully pushed lean management deep into their supply chain, they have generally done so on an individual firm-by-firm basis. HE designed a *collective* approach, motivating each supplier to share its innovations and process improvements with the entire supply chain, rewarding that supplier for doing so, and incentivizing each of the others to learn about and adopt the improvements themselves. In this way, HE turned its supplier base into a giant learning organization.

The Deployment Strategy

In *The Highways England Delivery Plan 2015–20*, HE spelled out how it intended to achieve its ambitious goals: "[We will] implement a Lean deployment strategy that will build a culture of continuous improvement throughout Highways England and its supply chain to deliver increased customer value and efficiency saving in support of the Strategic Business Plan."[3]

This strategy was built on the supply-chain initiative begun by the former Highways Agency. Over time, HE has honed its approach for deploying lean throughout its supply chain into four basic elements: 1) engaging the leaders of supplier companies; 2) developing lean capabilities in suppliers; 3) assuring sustainability of the suppliers' lean efforts; and 4) building an improvement engine.

1. Engaging the Leaders

Derek Drysdale, the former divisional director of lean improvement at HE and architect of its supply-chain initiative, told us that he was explicit with the leaders of both existing and potential suppliers that they were expected to be full partners with HE in continuous improvement: "You will not work with Highways England unless you are practicing lean principles."

According to Drysdale, adopting a lean approach to construction was often hard for suppliers:

> People are accustomed to doing things a certain way, often with a lot of firefighting. Lean is different. It is very systematic, involves a lot of planning, and people who are accustomed to working the old way often don't understand it at first. A supplier may "window dress" by engaging in a lean project or two, but make no real effort to make lean part of its culture.

In order to find suppliers with improvement-oriented leaders, HE prequalifies its suppliers for high-value projects using its Strategic Alignment Review Tool (StART). Although lean terminology is deliberately left out of StART, its approach and scoring regime aim to identify companies that already practice elements of continuous improvement. The StART process begins with an introductory briefing, after which the companies complete an extensive self-assessment that covers their leadership, how effectively they work with their customers and suppliers, the cost and quality of their work, their workforce diversity, and how they minimize their environmental impact. Then a team from HE conducts a site visit and prepares a feedback report along with the company's score. Although the resource-intensive StART process is reserved for suppliers on high-value projects, all potential contractors are rated on an evaluation scheme based 70 percent on quality and 30 percent on price, thus assuring from the outset that those selected are fairly well managed.

2. Developing Supplier Capabilities

For almost a decade, HE has been working with suppliers to encourage them to adopt lean construction methods and to collaborate on improvement. HE's goal is to create a community of companies practicing lean at a high level. Having its suppliers use a common vocabulary and set of management tools makes it easier to share improvements and to work together on lean projects that cut across the work of multiple suppliers.

HE provides its suppliers with extensive training opportunities—such as workshops, seminars, and webinars. It also has an extensive online library of articles, helpful templates for the various lean tools, write-ups of successful lean projects and innovative construction techniques (many with instructive YouTube videos), and other resources.

3. Assuring Sustainability of the Effort

New initiatives have a natural tendency to stagnate and falter after the initial energy wanes. As the novelty wears off, management moves on to the next new thing. Experience shows that lean is particularly susceptible to this tendency because after solving the early and obvious problems, further progress requires different ways of working and thinking and the development of a new management mindset and behavior. This involves considerable investment in education and training, significant changes in the organization's systems and the way people work, and sustained effort from leadership. In Drysdale's experience, the tipping point where lean becomes self-sustaining occurs when 70 percent of the people in an organization fully understand and embrace it.

To help its suppliers keep their lean efforts moving forward, HE developed the Highways England Lean Maturity Assessment (HELMA). This tool is used to evaluate where each supplier's lean effort stands and to identify next steps to deepen and broaden it. Twenty-six suppliers participate in the HELMA process. These include most of HE's major suppliers, many of which are large multinational companies. HELMA has ten areas of assessment:

1. Integration of lean in business strategy

2. Lean leadership and engagement

3. Deployment of management/lean infrastructure

4. Understanding customer value

5. Understanding of process and value streams

6. Use of methodologies and tools

7. Organizational coverage, activity, and capability

8. Performance improvement/benefit realization and delivery

9. Lean collaboration, climate, and culture

10. Supplier maturity

The HELMA process begins with the organization self-assessing and self-scoring its lean progress, followed by an external assessment visit from members of the HE lean team. The visits are typically two days in length and provide a forum for discussing the company's performance in each of these ten areas. The process ends with a feedback meeting, followed a week later by a written feedback report. The goal is to help each supplier develop a HELMA improvement plan to keep its lean initiative moving forward.

4. Creating the Improvement Engine

One of the biggest challenges was to invent a structure that would enable the supply chain, as a whole, to become a giant learning organization—one in which competitors share improvements with one another and lessons learned by one supplier are rapidly transferred to the others. The challenge was to think out how financial benefits from the higher performance could be distributed in a way that incentivized suppliers (many of whom are direct competitors) to make improvements, share those improvements with each other, and apply what they learn to future work. To see how this is done, take for example the £2 billion Managed Motorway Framework.

For the projects covered by this framework, HE works directly with five Tier 1 suppliers—large multinational construction companies that are capable of managing huge projects and organizing the work of all the lower-tier suppliers. Tier 1 suppliers were selected through a unique bidding process. Rather than bidding on specific projects, which is the norm in construction, their bids were for the rates (including "normal" profits) they would charge for specific classifications of labor, equipment, materials, and overhead—the components that make up every project. Large multiyear contracts were then assigned to each Tier 1 supplier. Historical performance data from similar projects were used as a starting point to negotiate each contract price based on existing standard practices.

A creative savings-sharing scheme rewards suppliers for improving on those standard practices and for sharing their learnings with each other. Any savings from the negotiated base price are split 40/60, with 40 percent going to HE and 60 percent going into a pool for *all* Tier 1 suppliers. The improved performance standard then becomes the new base standard for the next round of contracts. Because all of the Tier 1 suppliers need to meet the new higher standards, the 60-percent pool is shared using an interesting formula. Twenty percent of the savings goes to the Tier 1 supplier responsible for that contract, and the remaining 40 percent is divided equally among all five Tier 1 suppliers. In this way, every contractor has a stake in the improvements the other contractors make and in using these improvements on their own jobs as soon as possible.

In order to facilitate collaboration and learning between suppliers, HE recognized that it would be critical for all of them to work with the same lean techniques—that is, for them to speak the same language. Several lean construction tools that have proven particularly helpful are visual management, collaborative planning, and performance management. These techniques improve the coordination of jobs by making work plans and schedules visual and clear. They are particularly powerful when combined with co-location of select supplier personnel who, when working together, can pinpoint where to focus lean improvement projects for maximum impact. To assure that lessons learned from these lean projects are shared across the supply chain, HE developed an online Lean Project Tracker system. This database lists all the significant lean improvement projects undertaken by HE suppliers, with detailed descriptions that allow others to replicate them. Here are some examples:[4]

- A lean project in one highway maintenance region addressed the resurfacing productivity of the night shift on a particular repaving contract. Historically, the average had been 240 tons of paving put down per shift. The project achieved a 54 percent increase in resurfacing speed, resulting in a cost saving of £635,000 and a one-third reduction in completion time, which meant eighteen fewer overnight road closures on that contract.

- During a job on the M60 to upgrade the storm drainage system, a lean project explored the practicality of using precast (factory-made) concrete drainage chambers (storm-sewer basins under drainage grates) rather than the standard practice of setting up forms and casting the concrete structures in place. The project resulted in an estimated savings of £150,000 on the contract, including a 10 percent direct material cost savings, and a time-saving of approximately 7.5 days, while increasing quality and providing a safer work environment. The Lean Tracker thoroughly documented the new process for installing the chambers, listed a number of construction management tips, and even identified an appropriate supplier for the precast chambers.

■ It is an ongoing challenge to keep construction vehicles flowing smoothly through construction sites with a minimum of work disruption and vehicle-waiting time. One lean project took on this challenge for a job on a twenty-mile stretch of the busy M1 motorway. Site-access logistics were reconceptualized to optimize the flow of vehicles through the work areas while reducing disruptions due to the use of incorrect entry and exit points. Better planning meetings were introduced at the start of each shift during which the day's work was scheduled and the daily entry-exit plans were agreed upon. The improved job-site traffic flow allowed an increase in the number of concurrent activities being performed without negatively impacting productivity. The project's net savings were £1,058,680, with an additional £1,042,720 expected from applying the new practices to another job scheduled on a different stretch of the M1.

Over four hundred such projects have been documented in detail on the Lean Tracker.

HE also developed several other knowledge transfer systems for its suppliers. For example, hundreds of front-line employee improvement ideas have been documented and entered into the HE Knowledge Bank for other suppliers to see. Many of these entries incorporate YouTube clips so that the improved techniques and procedures can be more easily understood.

Highways England has saved hundreds of millions of pounds with its innovative supply-chain strategy. It estimates that for every £1 it has invested in its lean supply-chain initiative (e.g., training, resources, personnel, etc.), it has received £32 back in savings so far, and the improved methods promise to generate additional savings far into the future.

The primary lesson we can draw from the Highways England story is that continuous improvement does not stop at your organization's boundaries. In fact, we believe that some of today's greatest CI opportunities in government are in creating service-delivery ecosystems of public and private organizations learning together in ways that benefit all parties.

14

How Denver Became the Global Benchmark for Legalizing Marijuana

n November 2012, Colorado voters passed Amendment 64 to the state constitution. The amendment gave local governments in the state the right to either prohibit or regulate and license the cultivation, processing, testing, distribution, and consumption of recreational marijuana. Given that more than 60 percent of the citizens of Denver voted in favor of the amendment, Mayor Michael Hancock and the city council decided to proceed with the legalization and regulation of marijuana within city limits.

The amendment had set a tight deadline for the legalization process. The city had only eight months to create and pass the relevant laws and regulations, and another three months before it had to start accepting applications for licenses (there were seven different kinds specified in the amendment). It had to allow retail outlets to start opening three months after that.

In the best of circumstances, this would have been a tight timetable. But for legalizing marijuana there were no existing models to follow or learn from. Although a handful of states had legalized the medical use of marijuana, and a few others had decriminalized its possession in small quantities for personal use, it remained illegal nationwide to grow, process, stock, distribute, or consume it for recreational purposes. Denver would be the first major city to legalize all this, and it would need to pioneer every aspect of regulating, licensing, and policing the new marijuana supply chain. The lack of any models to follow meant the city would have to launch its initiative without understanding everything that would be involved. City authorities knew they would have to learn on the job, and learn fast. From the beginning, Mayor Hancock was quite public about this: "We don't know what we don't know." The marijuana industry's budding entrepreneurs were also having to learn how to operate in an environment that seemed to be changing on a daily basis.

The mayor and city council set some broad guidelines for how the regulations and operating requirements should be developed. The process would be completely transparent, all stakeholders would be involved in developing the system, and this system was to place particular emphasis on the needs and desires of the community. Complicating the upcoming discussions were the widely differing and strongly held views on what the licensing and enforcement laws should look like. The bywords for the legalization initiative became "robust regulation and strict enforcement." With all eyes on Denver, if the process didn't go well, the city's reputation would suffer.

Denver mobilized quickly. The mayor set up a marijuana "SWAT team" consisting of key individuals from departments that the new laws would affect; the city council set to work developing the Denver Retail Marijuana Code; and various task forces and committees worked on other issues. By December 2013, Mayor Hancock realized that the city needed a single point of contact to coordinate its response to all the marijuana-related issues that were expected to arise. He established the Office of Marijuana Policy (OMP) and appointed Ashley Kilroy, a lawyer working for the city, as its head. Kilroy's first hires included a data analyst, whose job it was to set up systems for tracking and making sense of what she expected to be a rapidly changing environment, and a communications specialist, who would help with the flood of media questions that she anticipated.

To organize the legalization process, Kilroy conceived what became known as the Denver Collaborative Model (DCM), which was designed to make the city "nimble, efficient, and effective" at addressing the still-unknown situations that would emerge from legalizing marijuana. The model was designed to rapidly identify problems, gather information, and modify existing policies or make new ones.

The DCM can be viewed as a set of concentric circles. In the center circle is the OMP, which at its peak had a staff of five. The next circle is the Coordinated Marijuana Policy Team (CMPT) consisting of one or two high-level representatives from each of the primary agencies that needed to be involved with the legalization process. These included

- the Denver Police Department (DPD), which would be enforcing the new regulations;

- the Denver Fire Department (DFD), which would be dealing with fire issues and conducting safety inspections;

- the Community Planning and Development Department, which would be involved in zoning decisions, building inspections, and ensuring marijuana operations were kept away from schools, day care centers, parks, and so on;

- the Department of Excise and Licenses (Denver Licensing), which would be responsible for developing and issuing the seven new types of licenses, conducting inspections, and issuing citations;

- the Department of Public Health and Environment, which would need to address the issues involved in growing (pesticides used, odor complaints, etc.) and processing (in which some hazardous petroleum-based chemicals were used as solvents), as well as any potential public health issues that emerged; and

■ the City Attorney's office.

For the first several years, the CMPT met weekly.

The next circle of the DCM encompassed more peripheral city agencies, including Treasury (mostly for taxation issues), Parks and Recreation (for consumption enforcement—no consumption would be allowed in public or in city parks), the Budget and Management Office (involved on both the revenue and expenses side), Denver 311 (which fielded thousands of marijuana-related calls), the Office of Children's Affairs (responsible for messaging about the dangers of marijuana to young brains), the Office of Behavioral Health, the Denver International Airport (potential marijuana smuggling was a concern), and the Department of Technical Service (for IT support and infrastructure).

The outer circle of the DCM was a series of standing meetings including a quarterly meeting with marijuana industry representatives to listen to its concerns and to get feedback on proposed regulatory changes; a quarterly meeting with the Colorado Marijuana Enforcement Division to share issues and coordinate responses; a quarterly meeting with the Colorado Department of Agriculture; and a monthly meeting with the governor's office. In addition, there were regularly scheduled telephone calls with various state and local agencies.

High-quality and timely information were central to the model's ability to allow the OMP to identify and respond rapidly to emerging issues. Getting this rapid feedback on what was happening in the field was where the people working on the front lines of marijuana issues came into play. The police officers, health inspectors, safety inspectors, and others who dealt directly with the public were in the best positions to spot new problems and emerging issues and to report them quickly to the OMP.

It is worth noting that without the DCM's capability to identify and respond rapidly to issues as they emerged, many important interventions would not have taken place until the issues created enough problems to show up in aggregate statistics or, worse yet, in the media. Also, in many cases this would have resulted in the response coming too late to alter the trajectory of the industry's development. As Kilroy pointed out, if the city hadn't been able to jump on issues immediately, "the toothpaste would be out of the tube" and many industry norms would be established by marijuana entrepreneurs rather than the city.

Ultimately, the DCM helped the city to manage a remarkably smooth transition to legalized recreational marijuana and a well-run marijuana industry. During the first four years, over 1,100 commercial marijuana licenses were issued with few problems, and a culture of responsible entrepreneurship and candid industry-regulator dialogue was established. This does not mean the legalization was problem free—indeed it could well have been derailed by some serious problems that arose. But the DCM ensured a rapid and thoughtful response to them, and it was able to keep the legalization effort nimble, yet always under control. Following are some examples of how this worked.

Shortly after Colorado's marijuana industry officially opened for business, there was a rash of hash oil explosions across the state, including a number in Denver. Also called cannabis oil, hash oil is a highly potent resinous oil extracted from marijuana with uses including smoking, vaping, cooking, and as an additive to edibles and drinks. Although it can be extracted safely under proper industrial conditions with the right solvents, fire inspectors found many people doing it at home on the cheap. They were cooking the oil out of ground marijuana leaves using butane vapor, which is highly explosive. And even in commercial operations, DFD safety inspectors were encountering dangerous "Franken-machines" (as several of our interviewees referred to them)—processing equipment cobbled together from assorted components. Because marijuana was still illegal nationally, commercially manufactured processing equipment that was UL (Underwriters Laboratories) safety-certified was not available. Exacerbating the danger was the location of many of the commercial hash oil processing operations. For zoning purposes, the city had initially classified marijuana bakeries as "Food Preparation and Sales." Consequently, many of these operations were located in dense retail environments. Something had to be done, and quickly. (Ironically, the problem had been flagged through the DCM by front-line workers even before the headline-grabbing explosions—which gave the problem even greater urgency.)

The OMP called a meeting, which included architects, engineers, and industry representatives. They quickly came up with a set of rules governing hash oil processing, including what equipment could be used. At the time, the fire department was sending inspectors to each facility and issuing operating permits on a case-by-case basis. Not only was this time consuming, but the inspectors did not have the expertise to understand the "customized" equipment. To put the system on a more solid footing, the decision was made to require each company to hire its own engineers, who would certify its equipment as safe, and only then would the DFD issue the needed permit. The DFD also developed standards for hash-oil extraction systems, which were later incorporated into the national standards for marijuana-processing equipment.

Over the next year, regulations tightened considerably on hash-oil extraction: it was made illegal to process the oil in unlicensed facilities (such as private houses); the equipment had to be a closed-loop system with (expensive) special hoods to capture butane vapors; and processing could only take place in Class 1 Division 1 rooms (rooms designed to be spark-free and properly ventilated so they could safely handle flammable liquids and gases). The zoning department, which had initially viewed marijuana bakeries as no different than bakeries making cupcakes and brownies, rezoned them as "industrial," and then, as the marijuana task force better understood the issues involved, as "heavy industrial."

Another early issue arose when inspectors reported seeing containers of pesticides carrying the warning "Unfit for human consumption" in growing operations. Were the pesticides safe to use? The problem was that federal agencies—the EPA, the FDA, and the USDA—regulated the use of pesticides and were the experts on what types could be used in what situations. With marijuana illegal at the federal level, the city could not expect help from any of them. Since marijuana was either smoked or consumed in food, the city decided that only pesticides approved for use in growing tobacco and food would be allowed when growing marijuana. The city was sued almost immediately, with the plaintiffs claiming that the city was acting outside its jurisdiction by regulating pesticides. Denver won the case.

The city also had to respond to potential food safety issues in the absence of any state or federal regulations. Here again, its front-line eyes and ears proved invaluable. Entrepreneurs were constantly testing the boundaries of the regulations and introducing new products. In particular, the DCM had to develop ways to quickly identify potentially harmful new products and recall them if necessary. New products that emerged included marijuana eye-drops, nose-drops, injectables, and "diamonds." When the first reports of diamonds came in, the OMP team asked itself, "What are diamonds?" Diamonds, it turned out, are highly potent crystals of super-pure THC, the active ingredient in cannabis. Also of concern was the fact that diamonds are made with pentane, a highly flammable gas.

At times, it seemed like the more problems the DCM solved, the more new ones popped up. The OMP soon discovered how creative people could be in getting around the rules. Amendment 64 allowed an individual to grow up to six marijuana plants for personal use without any licensing or inspection requirements. People began to combine their allowances to avoid being regulated. Reports began coming in of twelve people, say, in a house growing seventy-two plants without a license. Soon marijuana entrepreneurs were forming growing cooperatives to pool hundreds of allowances, renting warehouse space, and cultivating several thousand plants. These developments made it almost impossible for the DPD to enforce the six plants rule and were dangerous as they created large-scale growing centers that were unlicensed and uninspected. Again, the DCM worked as planned—the OMP quickly picked up on the issue and assembled a meeting of the people needed to work on a solution. The mayor and city council passed regulations that allowed a maximum of twelve plants in a private home, no matter how many people lived there, and a maximum of thirty-six plants per unit/area not specifically zoned for commercial marijuana activity.

Some indirect surprises popped up. Both the city and the power company were caught off guard by the jump in demand for electricity that was caused by the marijuana growing operations. By law, cannabis could only be grown in enclosed and locked spaces. For homeowners, this meant in special rooms or sheds, and for large commercial growers, this generally meant warehouses. The indoor growing took place under high-intensity lights, which consumed a great deal of electricity, and soon began to stress pockets of the grid and cause local power outages. Further complicating the problem, the transformers supplying the power to the converted warehouses were generally not rated for the electrical loads from hundreds or thousands of high-intensity growing lights. And with many of these old warehouses located in a floodplain, upgrading the electrical infrastructure would be more expensive and complicated. So the public works department and the utilities had a huge mess to sort out.

Another casualty of the increased power use was Denver's carbon reduction plan, which called for 80 percent of power to come from renewable sources by 2035. With nearly 4 percent of the city's electricity suddenly being consumed growing marijuana, the industry put a dent in the power company's and Denver's carbon reduction plans. In an effort to address this issue, the Denver Department of Public Health and Environment formed the Cannabis Sustainability Working Group in 2016 to hold regular stakeholder engagements in order to share best practices. A year later it published the *Cannabis Environmental Best Management Practices Guide*, which drew on experts across the country. One focus of the report was on the use of more energy-efficient and cooler lights. They would not only reduce the power needed for lighting, but they would also reduce the power needed for cooling because of all the heat generated by inefficient lamps. In 2018, the electricity used for marijuana production dropped for the first time, by an appreciable 8 percent.

Although the OMP and the Denver Collaborative Model have allowed the city to learn rapidly and, for the most part, safely carry out the wishes of its voters, new challenges continue to arise. The US Congress passed the 2018 Farm Bill with a provision that legalized the growing of hemp. Hemp is a valued industrial material with many applications, from rope and textiles to paper, plastics, and insulation. The problem is that hemp is the male version of the cannabis plant and only an expert can distinguish it from a marijuana plant. Legalized growing of hemp greatly complicates the regulation and oversight of growing recreational marijuana. It is much easier and cheaper to grow marijuana in a farm field than under artificial lights. With hemp now legal, and with it being all but impossible to distinguish between a field of hemp and a field of marijuana, enforcing the indoor-only growth rule has become a lot more complicated. Immediately, the city had to engage in a new round of "learning."

15

Denmark's MindLab and User-Centered Policy Innovation

Note: This chapter draws in part from an article we wrote for the *Journal of Government Financial Management*. We are grateful to the journal for permission to incorporate that material here.[1]

F ew things define the quality of leaders in government more, or have a greater impact on their constituents' lives, than the nature and effectiveness of the policies they create. Unfortunately, leaders often lack the policy-making tools, techniques, and training needed to make certain their policies accomplish their intended goals efficiently. As Otto von Bismarck, Germany's first chancellor, observed, "Laws are like sausages, it is better not to see them being made." He was referring to the wheeling and dealing, backroom horse-trading, and compromises that typically take place as laws are created. The process is not pretty, and it is frequently based more on politics and ideology than on facts and reason.

MindLab, an innovation unit within the Danish government, developed a creative way to incorporate CI into the country's policy-making process by using user-centered innovation and design thinking. Its novel approach shattered longstanding norms and promised to make policies more effective and easier to implement. MindLab's story is both interesting and instructive.

In 2002, the Danish Permanent Secretary (the highest nonpolitical administrator) of the (then) Ministry of Business Affairs spoke at the Copenhagen Business School. During his talk he emphasized that one of the ministry's primary missions was to help Danish businesses be more innovative. Afterward, several business professors asked him what the ministry was doing to make *itself* more innovative. As a direct result of this challenge, the ministry set up MindLab as its internal innovation unit.

Initially, MindLab focused on shaking up the way government went about its normal work. It provided a "creative space" where people could collaborate on difficult or politically charged issues with the help of a MindLab facilitator. The idea was to break people out of their normal culture of interest-driven meetings so they could engage in collective problem-solving.

MindLab's operating philosophy changed significantly in 2010. Under new leadership, MindLab shifted from challenging the system from the outside to working with government units to improve the system from the inside. At the same time, MindLab adopted the design thinking approach to innovation, which greatly enhanced its ability to understand the effects of the policies it was asked to study. This approach was built around a *deep dive*—an ethnographic study involving detailed firsthand observation of people interacting with a specific service or system. These ethnographic studies had two components. First, study teams would conduct extensive interviews with all key stakeholders, including the citizens impacted, the front-line staff and managers responsible for implementing the policy, and the high-level policymakers themselves. Second, team members would observe stakeholders as they dealt with various aspects of the issues being addressed by the policy or as they interacted or worked with the policy itself.

In spring 2013, the Ministry of Employment asked MindLab to evaluate a major new policy. The policy dealt with "early retirement," the term Denmark uses for the financial support given to citizens who cannot work because of mental or physical disabilities. The new policy was intended to fundamentally reform how the country dealt with these citizens, particularly those under the age of forty. The goal was to move early retirees back into the workforce. The thinking was that the new policy would not only save money, but enrich their lives.

The early retirement reforms were passed in late December 2012, with implementation to begin on January 1, 2013. Moving early retirees back into the workforce would require a major change in how local municipalities dealt with these clients. Traditionally, a social-service caseworker simply followed a set of guidelines to determine if a person met the criteria to receive early retirement benefits. If so, the needed paperwork would be filed, and the person would start receiving regular payments.

The new policy called for a case management approach in which representatives from all relevant local social service agencies would work collaboratively in cross-disciplinary teams in order to help clients make the shift back into the workforce. Each client's team consisted of six to nine civil servants: a coordinating caseworker from the Department of Employment; representatives from the family, social, and health departments; a physical therapist; a physician; a personal caseworker; and a secretary. The team was to meet with the client to review their case and develop a transition plan. With all the support agencies at the table, the thinking was that the client could get the help—whether it was physical therapy, training, education, a fitness course, or other—needed to successfully reengage in the workplace.

One of the major challenges these teams faced was finding jobs that their clients could perform. Because of their handicaps and limited work experience, it was unlikely they could succeed if thrust into traditional work environments. The first goal, therefore, was to find them an initial entry job, even if it was for only two hours per week or was modified to fit their capabilities. Once the clients were employed, their support teams would work to gradually expand their workplace abilities and enhance their jobs.

MindLab began its assessment of the effectiveness and impact of the new policy with an extensive ethnographic study in May 2013. Anna Sofie Jacobsen was assigned as the MindLab project lead. Her team included two MindLab colleagues and two staffers from the Ministry of Employment. One of these staffers, Jakob Heltoft, had been instrumental in formulating the initial policy.

Many of the problems the ethnographic study identified were caused by a combination of two factors. The first was the lack of a fully thought-through implementation plan. The task of implementing the reforms was left to the ninety-eight municipalities across Denmark, which were provided with little or no guidance and an extremely short timeline to implement the new policy. (Recall that the law was passed in late December and took effect on January 1.)

The second issue was the lack of understanding by the national-level policymakers of important local-level realities. For example, during the ethnographic study, the assessment team observed many of the cross-disciplinary teams working with their clients. While some meetings functioned as intended, most were chaotic and stressful. The team members were unaccustomed to collaborating and had been given no guidelines to follow. Furthermore, they came from different departments with conflicting interests, which often led to fruitless power games as the cross-disciplinary teams hashed out execution issues—often in front of clients. And the clients, who had come to the meetings seeking help, were often treated rudely and humiliated.

When Heltoft saw how the client meetings were playing out, he was shocked. What had seemed to be a conceptually brilliant approach when the policy was being developed was simply not working.

Another surprising implementation-related issue the team discovered was a shortfall in the caseworkers' interpersonal skills. An important part of the reform was to have each client personally involved in developing their own transition plan. Prior to the reform, the "client" was little more than a welfare application form that the caseworkers processed remotely. But the reforms required them to work directly with clients. Though caseworkers were typically professional social workers who had taken classes in how to work with mentally and/or physically challenged clients, some had never practiced these skills; others had lost them after years of focusing primarily on paperwork. They needed a refresher course.

The ethnographic study also found that even very minor issues could derail a client's progress on moving into the workforce. For example, one client who was granted a few weeks of occupational therapy to improve their physical ability to do a job could not afford the training shoes needed for therapy. Another client was not performing well at work because of a lack of sleep due to a bad mattress. Many municipalities set up modest budgets and streamlined funding processes to easily address such issues. Fixing these seemingly small problems made a big difference.

Once all these and other early issues were identified and addressed, the new early retirement policy proved highly effective in achieving the ministry's financial goals. Not only did it stop the rising cost of early retirement, but it actually reversed the trend (see Figure 15.1).

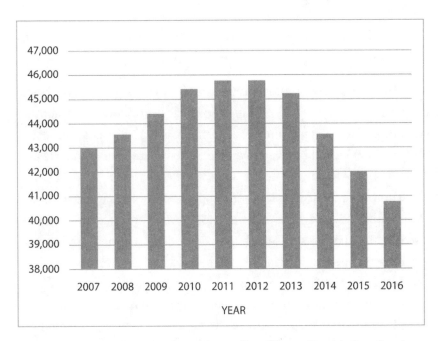

Figure 15.1: Early Retirement Expenditures (in millions of Danish Krone)

But another outcome from the MindLab study would have a much broader and longer lasting impact.

MindLab's assessment of the early retirement reform highlighted serious shortcomings in the way the ministry formulated policies. Had a field study been incorporated into the process, most of the problems identified could have been anticipated and eliminated while the original policy was being developed. Some of the staff at both MindLab and the ministry had already been informally discussing the need to improve how policies were made, so when the study so clearly confirmed this need, the work on creating a better process began in earnest. Ultimately, MindLab's new approach was built on three principles:

1. Know the target group and the front-line staff responsible for implementing the policy, and involve them early in co-creating it.

2. Include implementation issues in the policy creation process from the beginning.

3. Conduct regular follow-up assessments and continue to make improvements in the policy.

MindLab's new policy development process had five steps: 1) research, 2) analysis, 3) ideation, 4) testing, and 5) implementation. Once the new policy was in place, the policy loop (shown in Figure 15.2) kicked in and the entire cycle was repeated on a regular basis to refine and improve the policy.

The Ministry of Employment approved the new approach, and MindLab held a workshop to train 150 ministry managers in its use. At the time of our last research trip to MindLab, the new approach to making policies had spread to the Ministry of Economics, and several other ministries were considering its adoption.

Over time, MindLab refined its policy-reviewing process considerably. If the new policy loop was to be widely deployed throughout

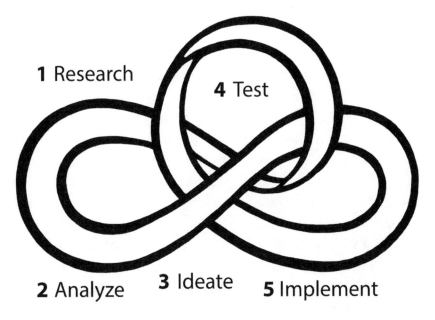

1 Research

4 Test

2 Analyze   **3 Ideate**   **5 Implement**

Figure 15.2: MindLab's Policy Loop

Danish government, the ethnographic study process—originally used to study only major national reforms—would have to be significantly streamlined. Originally, MindLab had developed and successfully used a nine-day framework for this process, but it soon realized that a shorter three-day version was more appropriate for smaller initiatives and ongoing follow-ups.

MindLab's experience shows that even at the policymaking level, a front-line perspective can play a pivotal role. Whatever the underlying political values, creating policy from a distance, without much understanding of the practical issues involved, greatly reduces the chances that it will achieve its objectives and can create significant unintended consequences. And rarely do new policies work perfectly from the outset. Conditions change. Like any other aspect of an organization, policies need ongoing adjustment and improvement throughout their existence. Policy making is much more effective when those making the policies learn how to effectively seek and use front-line input.

Epilogue

On May 1, 2018, MindLab was shut down. The government's innovation priority changed to "digitally reform Denmark's civil service."[2] Although MindLab had tried to reposition itself to help with this digital transformation, as Thomas Prehn, its last director, admitted, "it would have taken a few years to change design thinking consultants into more of a transformation team."[3] The prime minister set up a new Disruption Task Force to spearhead the digital initiative, and seven of MindLab's eighteen employees were transferred to the new ten-person unit.

MindLab was the original policy innovation laboratory, and it was an international catalyst of public-sector innovation. It helped the UK, Brazil, the Netherlands, Canada, and Uruguay set up their own policy labs. It has even worked with the EU and UN to promote public-sector innovation. It was copied in many nations, including in the US by the Office of Personnel Management (OPM), which set up the OPM Innovation Lab in Washington, DC, and in Singapore with its Human Experience Lab. In Denmark, MindLab had a profound impact on government operations. According to Chritian Bason, who headed it from 2007 to 2014, "a lot of municipalities, local government bodies, and state administrations work with user engagement and collaborative innovation methods now. They may not call it co-design, or use other innovation terms, but there's been a major shift in how organizations think and work."[4]

In an interview, Thomas Prehn gave his perspective on the forces behind the shutdown of MindLab: "There is a time for everything, and it was time for something different. Very frankly, this was about being able, as a politician, to promote your politics."[5]

We left our study of MindLab with mixed feelings. On the one hand, it had pioneered some potentially game-changing concepts for policy-makers and had left an impressive global legacy. On the other hand, because it remained a standalone unit, it made itself an easy target for elimination whenever there was a change in government leadership.

CONCLUSION
How to Get Started

After reading this book, the prospect of creating a front-line–driven CI program may seem a bit daunting, particularly if you are a low-level manager in charge of a small group. Certainly, you have a lot to learn, but this should not stop you from getting started. It is usually not very difficult to make significant progress relatively quickly, especially if your group has not previously engaged in any serious front-line–driven improvement effort. Typically, there is a lot of low-hanging fruit because many processes and work practices have never been examined carefully and are ripe for improvement. We see an example of how this works in the early steps taken by the horticultural crew of the Parks and Trees division of the city of Fredericton, the capital of New Brunswick, Canada.

Getting Started in Fredericton, New Brunswick

Shortly after a CI training session, the horticultural crew was discussing where to apply the concepts they had just learned to make some improvements. They quickly zeroed in on the process used to water the flower and plant beds along city streets during the summer—a job that was labor intensive, costly, and inefficient.

For one thing, the city was using a five-ton tanker truck for the job, and driving this truck required a special class of license. Only a handful of full-time employees had such a license, and while they were away driving, they would often have to leave temporary workers, usually college students, unsupervised for long periods. Furthermore, watering plants is a time-sensitive process, but because no scheduled routes or procedures had been established, the plants were being tended at inconsistent intervals and given varying amounts of water.

In addition, the watering process involved a lot of unproductive time. When the truck needed refilling, it had to return to the central depot where it took twenty minutes to fill it from a hose. And because the filtered and chlorinated city water was low in nutrients, fertilizer had to be added to it. An average day of watering involved three hours of driving back and forth to the central depot, plus an hour and forty minutes on top of that to fill and refill the truck. The cumbersome process required a great deal of overtime.

After some brainstorming, the team proposed buying a trailer with a five-hundred-gallon water tank that could be towed behind one of the department's pickup trucks. The pickups did not require special licenses to drive and were much more fuel efficient. To avoid having to return to the central depot to refill the tank, the team suggested purchasing a high-speed pump that could be carried in the back of the pickup so the tank could be filled from the St. John River, which ran through the middle of the city and had multiple access points. Not only was it much faster and more convenient to fill the tank this way, but the river water had no chlorine and contained natural nutrients that eliminated the need to add fertilizer. Using river water also reduced the city's water bill because the watering crews would no longer be using potable water.

The team also developed a new watering procedure that both saved time and ensured that all the plants would receive the correct amount of water. In addition, they purchased new software that allowed them to calculate the most efficient watering routes. The new procedure could be performed entirely by temporary employees, allowing the regular staff to focus on more value-adding and higher-skilled work. And because the procedure was much more efficient, the need for overtime was eliminated.

Other than the group's strong improvement orientation, there was no magic in the horticultural crew members' early improvement efforts. First, they did not use sophisticated techniques to choose their initial improvement project; they simply chose a task that was causing them significant difficulty. Second, the problem was relatively straightforward to analyze. The crew was very familiar with the existing watering practices and could easily assemble most of the information about times and costs. Third, there was no single home-run solution—the solution was a collection of smaller ideas. Fourth, while some investment was needed—such as in the tank trailer, pump, and software—none of the expenditures required complex calculations to justify. Their payback periods were well within a single season. Fifth, the solution came together in pieces, with each new idea building on previous ones. The idea to use a watering trailer eliminated the problem of tying up the tanker truck and permanent staff, but it required a lot more trips back to the central depot. Drawing water from the river solved that problem and had the added benefit of saving on fertilizer. The routing software and other ideas followed until they added up to an innovative and more practical process for watering the city's plants. Once again, there was no magic here—just some initial training and creative brainstorming, along with modest support from management.

Start with Where You Are

So, where do you start? You start with where you are. Where you are in your organization; where you are in terms of support from your superiors and the rest of your organization; where you are with your knowledge about CI; and where the unit you are responsible for stands in terms of its CI capability and resources for improvement.

Front-Line Leaders

If you are a front-line manager or supervisor with limited authority and little CI experience, you should start with your own work habits and education. Become a student of both continuous improvement *and leadership*. Read, observe, take courses, attend conferences, and listen to podcasts and webinars. Look for like-minded individuals in your organization and learn together. Stay alert for professional associations with relevant events and speakers, even if they are primarily private-sector groups. And—our favorite—go and see how others are practicing CI, from both the technical and the leadership standpoints. During your visits, be sure to talk with front-line supervisors and managers, as well as front-line employees, so that you can learn about front-line–driven improvement firsthand.

While you are building your own knowledge, start planning your strategy to build a front-line–driven culture in your group. Begin with where your team members are. Ask them which problems and difficulties they see as most significant: What are the biggest time wasters, the most frequent mistakes and sources of frustration, and the non–value-adding activities that the group should stop doing? Concentrate on things that are within the control of your team. How can the work be made easier? Post the issues they identify on a whiteboard or flip chart where everyone can see them, and then discuss what the group can do about them. Begin by focusing on *quick wins*—changes that are easy to implement and have discernable, even if modest, benefits. One of the biggest mistakes a team can make at this stage is to take on a large issue in its entirety. If your team wants to work on such a project, discuss how it can be broken up into smaller tasks that can be completed over a reasonable timeframe. Post the actions to be taken and assign responsibility for them. The following week, review the results of these actions, decide on follow-up actions, and assign responsibility for these. Make sure to acknowledge progress as it happens.

Once your people are engaged in improvement activity and experience the benefits from it, you have the foundation of a CI process to build upon. Look for appropriate training opportunities that are available through your organization. Are there improvement experts in your organization who can help you? As your employees become accustomed to improving and expand their skills and knowledge, start having them identify and take on more complex problems. To get ideas for new avenues of improvement, you might want to visit your unit's customers within the larger organization and ask them how you could support them better.

Keep this cycle going. As your group improves performance and becomes more innovative, your people will have more pride in their work, enjoy it more, and grow as individuals. You will be well on your way to creating your own pocket of excellence.

Mid-Level Managers

As a mid-level manager in charge of a larger group, you are in a different situation than a front-line leader. Although you have more resources and authority to draw upon, you must also work through others reporting to you. As such, you cannot achieve very much unless you recruit the managers and supervisors reporting to you to help in your effort to transform your group. The first step will typically involve two related actions: acquiring the CI knowledge you will need and assessing your group—particularly its managers and supervisors—to determine what will be needed to get front-line CI improvement activity started.

When building your knowledge and skills, however you choose to do this, invite your key managers and staff to join you. Because of your position, you may have more options available than we discussed for front-line leaders. And depending upon your authority and budget, hiring a consultant or coach may also be an option. As with the front-line managers, study visits are a very effective learning tactic. Seeing is believing. Take your managers and supervisors to visit other government operations with front-line–driven CI. If there are none in your area, look for examples in the private sector. Site visits can be particularly powerful after some initial training, because at that point your people will have a better understanding of CI and get more out of the visits. Encourage them to learn from the experiences of their counterparts in the host organizations. And before returning home from each visit, debrief. Discuss what they saw and learned, and talk about how it can be applied to your own group's CI effort.

Concurrent with your knowledge-development work, start assessing how ready your people are for a CI initiative. Make time at a regular departmental meeting to discuss CI and how it might work for the group. Hold one-on-one conversations with your key managers. Some of them may well have prior experience with CI, which may have been good or may have been bad. Find out, and find out why. It should be enlightening. Be prepared to hear hesitation, particularly from those who have experienced only management-driven CI initiatives. Explain to them how front-line–driven CI is different and what it means for their roles in the initiative. And don't forget to talk with your front-line supervisors and maybe even some of their staff. Their thoughts will provide you with additional perspectives.

When you are ready to deploy your CI effort, don't rush it. Your organization and its people require time to adjust to an improvement-oriented way of thinking and working. You might want to start with a pilot. Ideally this would include a few carefully chosen first-level supervisors and their immediate managers. They should have good leadership skills and be excited about creating front-line improvement in their units. Make certain they have access to good training for themselves and their people, the support needed to set up their improvement systems, and a modest budget. Drop in on some of their idea meetings. Clear your visit with their manager and invite that manager to join you. Look to quickly identify and correct issues that emerge in order to ensure that your pilot areas are successful, and talk about that success with your other managers and supervisors. Discuss what was learned—what worked, what didn't, and why. Encourage the pilot manager and supervisors to share their stories, including specific examples of improvements and their impact.

As you look to roll out your full CI initiative, it will go much better if you use a coalition-of-the-willing approach. Start with interested volunteers, rather than mandating compliance, and make sure they have all the support they need to be successful. Early on, allow your managers and supervisors to opt in as they feel ready to take on the change. The success of the earlier adopters will encourage others to join the coalition. Only when the initiative is well-established should you put much energy into the laggards.

Once you are on your way, continue to learn, experiment, and learn more. And don't forget to highlight successes and celebrate them with your people. Finally, throughout the whole implementation process, be sure to *manage up*—frame your CI initiative in terms that align with your boss's goals and vision, and keep them appraised of the progress your group makes. Maybe even invite your own boss to attend one of your front-line idea meetings with you.

Higher-Level Managers

For higher-level managers, much of how to get started mirrors our advice to middle managers, but it is contextually different because the challenges you face are much more encompassing. Your goal to dramatically boost your organization's performance and responsiveness by embedding CI at the front-line level is more about leading organization-wide change than it is about the specifics of CI. Essentially, you are trying to shift your organization's culture. Because you need to work through a bureaucracy with many layers of management and whose different units may have divergent interests, one challenge you face is to get managers at all levels of your organization on board. And by the very nature of the outcome you seek—an empowered workforce taking initiative to make improvements—you cannot simply dictate the change. You need to convince and inspire your leaders and staff to join you in the transformation effort.

Your starting point is similar to that of middle managers in that it comprises three elements: getting yourself up to speed in terms of the knowledge you will need about CI and leading change; inspiring and informing your leadership team so they are excited about the upcoming change; and assessing your organization with an eye for what needs to be changed and what assets are in place that might prove useful in doing so. The differences are that you are working at a higher level and are dealing with more complexity, but you also have more assets to draw upon.

The approach you take depends upon your personal style and the context in which you lead. The same general tactics that we discussed for middle managers are open to you, but your authority opens more options. The most critical factor is to get the members of your leadership team behind the effort. Without their active involvement, your initiative will not get very far. Make your CI initiative part of every important conversation you have with members of your leadership team. Put discussion of progress on the transformation of your organization at the top of the agenda for regular leadership team meetings. You may well want help from outside consultants, but don't become too dependent on them. Make certain the knowledge and skills needed to launch and maintain front-line–driven CI are transferred to your people.

We conclude this book with a profound sense of optimism. What our study revealed gives the lie to what many people take for granted—that by their very nature government operations must be inefficient. We found many previously underperforming units whose leaders had transformed them into high performers, with some of them becoming as efficient as the best companies in the private sector. And they were able to do this while working within the normal constraints of government—with its extensive checks and balances, diverse stakeholders, complex mission, and goals that often transcend narrow financial interests. The special insight of these leaders was that front-line–driven improvement is almost perfectly designed for the public sector and that it is a powerful force for change.

We hope their stories, and this book, will inspire you to get started creating your own high-performing corner of government.

NOTES

Introduction

1 Some of these were T-Groups, Organizational Development, Quality Circles, Theory Z, Total Quality Management (TQM), Business Process Reengineering (BPR), Lean, Management by Objectives, Six Sigma, and even Lean Six Sigma.

2 This research is reported on in our book *The Idea-Driven Organization: Unlocking the Power in Bottom-Up Ideas* (San Francisco: Berrett-Koehler Publishers, 2014).

Chapter 1

1 *Encyclopedia Britannica* online, s.v. "Hoover Commission," April 11, 2013, https://www.britannica.com/topic/Hoover-Commission-United-States -government; *New York Times*, "Hoover Commissions Sought Government Reforms," October 21, 1964, 42.

2 J. Peter Grace, *Burning Money: The Waste of Your Tax Dollars* (New York: Macmillan, 1984).

3 Congressional Budget Office and General Accounting Office, "Analysis of the Grace Commission's Major Proposals for Cost Control" (Washington, DC: Congress of the United States, February 1984).

4 "The National Performance Review and Other Government Reform Initiatives: An Overview, 1993–2001," Congressional Research Service, Library of Congress, updated June 4, 2001.

5 David Osborne and Ted Gaebler, *Reinventing Government: How the Entrepreneurial Spirit Is Transforming the Public Sector* (Reading, MA: Addison-Wesley, 1992).

Chapter 2

1 *Lean* is a widely-used approach to CI that is derived from the Toyota Production System.

2   A *value-stream map* is a process flowchart that highlights critical performance metrics at each stage to help users focus improvement efforts where
they will have the most impact.
3   For more data and examples, see *The Idea-Driven Organization: Unlocking the
Power in Bottom-Up Ideas,* by Alan Robinson and Dean Schroeder (San Francisco: Berrett-Koehler, 2014).
4   Shigeo Shingo, *The Sayings of Shigeo Shingo: Key Strategies for Plant Improvement* (Portland, OR: Productivity Press, 1987), 18.

Chapter 3

1   Fred Luthans, Richard Hodgetts, and Stuart Rosenkrantz, *Real Managers*
(Cambridge, MA: Gollinger, 1988), 1.
2   Paul Schroeder, interview with authors, September 27, 2020.
3   Schroeder interview.
4   For a more complete explanation in the context of front-line ideas, see Chapter 3 in our book *Ideas Are Free: How the Idea Revolution Is Liberating People
and Transforming Organizations* (San Francisco: Berrett-Koehler, 2006). For a
broader explanation in the context of creativity as a whole, see *Punished by
Rewards* by Alfie Kohn (New York: Houghton Mifflin, 1993).
5   For more on this topic, see "On the Social Psychology of Agency Relationships: Lay Theories of Motivation Overemphasize Extrinsic Reward," by
Chip Heath, in *Organizational Behavior and Human Decision Processes* 78,
no. 1 (April 1999): 25–62.
6   Daniel Pink, *Drive: The Surprising Truth About What Motivates Us* (New York:
Riverhead Books, 2011).

Chapter 4

1   Aaron Wildavsky, *Speaking Truth to Power: The Art and Craft of Policy Analysis*
(Boston: Little, Brown, and Company, 1979), 42.
2   We use the term *vision* at the front-line level to refer to what some might
call a *goal*. Both terms deal with a desired future result, but there is an
important distinction between them. A vision is more substantive in
terms of its role in making major long-term strategic changes in an
organization.

Chapter 5

1   Alan G. Robinson and Dean M. Schroeder, "Employee Engagement That
Works: Continuous Improvement in New Brunswick," *Journal of Government
Financial Management* 64, no. 3 (Fall 2015): 19–23.

2   The *Balanced Scorecard* is an approach to cascading goals down an organization that balances leading indicators with current performance measures.
See *The Balanced Scorecard*, by Kaplan and Norton (Boston: Harvard Business School Press, 1996). Lean Six Sigma, which merges the concepts of lean
and Six Sigma, will be discussed more in Chapter 10.

Chapter 6

1   This story is told in more detail in *Ideas Are Free: How the Idea Revolution
Is Liberating People and Transforming Organizations*, by us (Oakland, CA:
Berrett-Koehler, 2006). See pages 208–213.
2   Robert Chin and Kenneth Benne, "General Strategies for Effecting Changes
in Human Systems." In Warren G. Bennis, Kenneth D. Benne, and Robert
Chin (Eds.), *The Planning of Change* (New York: Holt, Rinehart & Winston,
1969).

Chapter 8

1   This website can be viewed at www.codot.gov/business/
process-improvement/lean-everyday-ideas.
2   This website can be viewed at https://www.codot.gov/business/
process-improvement/idea-cards.

Chapter 9

1   Frank B. Gilbreth and L. M. Gilbreth, "Process Charts," paper presented at
the annual meeting of the American Society of Mechanical Engineers, New
York, December 5–9, 1921, p. 3.
2   John Shook, *Managing to Learn* (Cambridge, MA: Lean Enterprise Institute,
2008).

Chapter 10

1   PDCA, sometimes referred to as the Deming or Shewhart cycle, is a
common basic problem-solving framework.
2   A Pareto chart displays the frequency of occurrence of different problems.
It is used to prioritize improvement efforts.
3   Recall that Results Washington is the unit responsible for championing CI
throughout Washington State government; for more on this story and the
problem-solving lessons to be learned from it, see our article, "Solving the
Unsolvable: How to Address Complex Politically Charged Transorganizational Problems," *Organizational Dynamics* 46, 4 (Fall 2017): 212–219.

4   Robinson and Schroeder, "Solving the Unsolveable," 214.

5   Mike Rother and John Shook, *Learning to See: Value-Steam Mapping to Create Value and Eliminate Muda* (Cambridge, MA: The Lean Enterprise Institute, 2003).

6   Ken Watanabe, *Problem Solving 101: A Simple Book for Smart People* (New York: Penguin Books 2009).

Chapter 11

1   Daniel Jones, once a professor there, was co-author of the seminal books that introduced the world to lean: *The Machine That Changed the World* (New York: Free Press, 1990), and *Lean Thinking: Banish Waste and Create Wealth in Your Corporation* (New York: Free Press, 1996).

2   The Theory of Constraints was developed by Eliyahu Goldratt and introduced in his 1984 book *The Goal: A Process of Ongoing Improvement* (Great Barrington, MA: North River Press, 1984).

Chapter 12

1   Office of the Chief Administrative Officer, "Vision 2051," York Region, 11, https://www.york.ca/wps/portal/yorkhome/yorkregion/yr/seniormanagement /officeofthechiefadministrativeofficer/.

Chapter 13

1   Alan G. Robinson and Dean M. Schroeder, "A New Paradigm in Government Purchasing: Highways England and Its Continuously Improving Supply Chain," *Journal of Government Financial Management* 65, no. 4 (Winter 2016–17): 38–44.

2   £1 was approximately $1.3 at the time.

3   Highways England, "Highways England Delivery Plan 2015–2020," Corporate Report, Gov.UK, March 26, 2021, 54, https://www.gov.uk/government /publications/highways-england-delivery-plan-2015-2020.

4   These examples are drawn from the Highways England Lean Tracker, https://kol.withbc.com/HA-Lean/, December 7, 2021.

Chapter 15

1   Alan G. Robinson and Dean M. Schroeder, "How Leaders Can Create Policy That Actually Works," *Journal of Government Financial Management* 66, no. 4 (Winter 2017–18), 36–41.

2   "How Denmark Lost Its MindLab: The Inside Story," Apolitical, June 5, 2018, https://apolitical.co/solution_article/how-denmark-lost-its-mindlab-the -inside-story/.

3   "How Denmark Lost Its MindLab."

4   "How Denmark Lost Its MindLab."

5   "How Denmark Lost Its MindLab."

ACKNOWLEDGMENTS

This book would not have come about without the help of a lot of people. Some inspired us, others gave us advice or opened doors for us, and a great many generously gave their time to share their experiences and thinking with us.

There are too many people to acknowledge individually, but a number deserve special mention.

Gary Vansuch, Director of Process Improvement at the Colorado Department of Transportation played a pivotal role in initially drawing us into the research that became this book. He was always willing to act as a sounding board for our ideas and to introduce us to leaders who proved to be key contacts for our work. We met him during the early days of his Transportation Lean Forum, which has quietly and steadily grown into a global force promoting continuous improvement in the public sector.

Another person we are particularly grateful to is Jane Washburn, Chief of Strategy Management in the government of New Brunswick in Canada. New Brunswick was the first full-blown government-wide continuous improvement system we encountered, and it inspired us in the early stages of our research. A special thanks also to Monique Boudreau and Monique Vautour of Francophone Sud in New Brunswick for sharing their improvement journeys so openly with us.

Wendy Korthuis-Smith and Inger Brinck, two former directors of Results Washington, and their staffs gave us full support and opened doors across Washington State government for us. We are particularly grateful to two of the consultants in their office for the time they spent with us: Stew Henderson, who worked with us for several months to educate us about the complexity of the oyster farm closure problem and the amazingly creative way in which it was eventually solved; and Holly Jensen who helped us in so many ways.

In the city of Denver, we are grateful to Mayor Michael Hancock for the time he spent with us, his welcoming attitude, and the freedom he gave us to probe and ask questions. Brian Elms of Peak Academy greatly influenced our early thinking about CI in government. Stacie Loucks and Ashley Kilroy, both directors of Denver Licensing, and Melissa Wiley of Peak Academy were extremely generous with their time and very helpful.

The CI office of York regional government in Canada was always welcoming. Ted Burley was our guide as we tried to understand the unique culture of York regional government and how it had come about. He, Joanne Armstrong, and Michelle Adlam were extremely open with us, organized dozens of interviews, and went out of their way to arrange for us to experience an ILab workshop firsthand.

At the Royal Mint, we owe special thanks to Leighton John and Tony Baker, who so patiently explained the Mint's complex systems for continuous improvement and coordinated numerous interviews with front-line leaders and employees.

Rob Woods, former head of Arizona's Government Transformation Office, and now the state's Director of the Department of Revenue, was extremely helpful to us, as were Kismet Weiss, Leader of the Office of Continuous Improvement in the Arizona Department of Transportation, and Eric Jorgensen, Director of Arizona's Motor Vehicle Division.

Derek Drysdale of Highways England was also particularly helpful, as were Steven Greenhalgh, Katie Jones, and Neal Symmons. Their unique approach took a while for us to grasp, but they were all very patient with us.

We would also like to thank Julie Baker and Justin Doran of the Parks and Trees Division of the city of Fredericton, New Brunswick, for sharing the story of their improvement work with us.

We are grateful to the late Harry Kenworthy of QPIC, who so graciously let each of us attend one of his lean seminars and who was always happy to hear from us, offer us words of encouragement, and provide us with introductions.

As we pulled the book together, we had the amazingly supportive staff at Berrett-Koehler Publishers on our team. We owe a huge debt to Steve Piersanti, our editor, whose wisdom and insightful advice helped us clarify our message to make this a much better book. All throughout the publication process, it was a real pleasure to deal with consummate professionals who always sought our input and collaboration, even though they knew a lot more than we did!

And finally, we could not have gone on this seven-year journey without the patience and support of our life partners. To Margaret and Kate, we can only say a profound thank you! Another family member who deserves special recognition is Alan's mother, Gwen Robinson. She has been our writing coach, grammarian, editor, and occasional style arbiter on many projects over the years, and she played her usual key role in this book, too.

INDEX

ABOUT THE AUTHORS

Alan Robinson

Shortly after arriving at the University of Massa-chusetts as an assistant professor in the mid 1980s, Alan Robinson's career took an unexpected turn. His background—he had a BA/MA in mathematics from Cambridge University and a newly minted PhD in Operations Research from Johns Hopkins University—had prepared him well for modeling business problems mathematically, but he was beginning to realize that this approach was losing its relevance.

At the time, leading Japanese companies were starting to domi-nate their Western counterparts, selling vastly superior products at much lower prices. No one seemed to understand completely why these companies were performing so well, and Alan was curious. He decided to go to Japan to see for himself. Over the next few years, he did three historical research projects in that country, interviewing many Japanese managers and leaders who had witnessed the trans-formation or played a role in it. Perhaps more importantly, he studied the management of more than forty Japanese companies firsthand. They were operating in a totally different manner from anything he had ever seen or even conceived of before.

The most striking difference was the emphasis that Japanese leaders put on *kaizen,* or continuous improvement. What partic-ularly impressed Alan were the incredible numbers of ideas these companies were getting from their employees and how much they valued employee engagement in improvement. Alan began teaching the ideas to his students, speaking to conferences and professional groups, and working with early adopters in the business world.

During this time, he was fortunate to meet Dr. Shigeo Shingo, one of the co-developers of the Toyota Production System, who would have an enormous influence on his thinking. During a dinner, Shingo asked Alan how he could get his ideas in front of American university students, because they were the future. The result was *Modern Approaches to Manufacturing Improvement,* Alan's 1990 book with Shingo. According to the Society of Manufacturing Engineers (SME), it "remains a must-read for anyone interested in lean."

Ever since, Alan has continued to study and work with organizations all over the world, learning more about performance improvement, creativity, and innovation. His teaching, research, consulting, and writing all interact and cross-fertilize. His work has taken him into more than thirty countries on four continents.

Some of his more well-known books include

- *Corporate Creativity* (co-authored with Sam Stern), which was named Book of the Year by the Academy of Human Resource Management and which was a finalist in the *Financial Times*/Booz Allen & Hamilton Global Best Business Book Awards.

- *Vos Idées Changent Tout* (co-authored with Isaac Getz). In his preface to the German edition of this book, Heinrich von Pierer, President and CEO of Siemens AG, called this "an important book on a topic that is fundamental to every business."

- Two books with Dean Schroeder. *Ideas Are Free* was a global study of high-performing idea systems in more than 150 organizations in 17 countries. A syndicated columnist for Scripps Howard, Paul Tulenko, wrote this about the book: "I rate this book 5 1/2 stars, a first in this category. It's that powerful. (Only the Bible and the Constitution receive 6 stars.).*" The Idea-Driven Organization* was the result of five more years of research in an entirely new set of organizations. According to #1 *New York Times* best-selling business author Marshall Goldsmith, the book "is so reasonable that the magnitude of its change message is easy to miss."

Robinson has advised more than three hundred companies in thirty countries on how to improve their performance. Some of his more well-known clients have included the Federal Reserve Bank, GE, Kraft, Lucent Technologies, Interbrew, IKEA, MassMutual, NBTY, the US Navy, UBS, Alcan, Volkswagen, Standard & Poor's, *The Washington Post*, Heineken, Bose, Medtronic, AIG, the Cleveland Clinic, the Massachusetts General Hospital, Schneider Electric, the Brookhaven National Laboratory, Raytheon, Baptist Memorial Health Care, Liberty Mutual, and Allianz.

Along the way, Alan has also taught at St. Petersburg Technical University in Russia, the Athens Laboratory of Business Administration in Greece, the Jagiellonian University in Poland, the University of Porto in Portugal, the Hanoi Business School, and Tianjin University in China.

He is currently on the faculty of the Isenberg School of Management at the University of Massachusetts.

Dean Schroeder

Dean Schroeder's fascination with innovation and improvement started early. As a pre-teen paper carrier, he was constantly experimenting with better, faster ways to complete his route. After completing his degree in mechanical engineering (with an industrial engineering focus) from the University of Minnesota, Schroeder worked as an engineer designing the layout of manufacturing operations and introducing new technologies.

After completing his Master of Business Administration at the University of Montana, Schroeder took on the task of turning around a failing foundry. This is where he learned the power of the front lines. As the general manager, and with the help of a lot of improvement ideas from his employees, he led an effort that resulted in a 250 percent increase in production and an 80 percent decrease in defects in eight weeks. Schroeder went on to lead several additional organizational start-ups and transformations before returning to school for his advanced degree. During this period, Schroeder's interest in government operations was sparked when he was appointed to the Governor of Minnesota's Private Industry Council.

While at the University of Minnesota for his doctorate from the Carlson School of Management, Schroeder's course of study included classes from the Hubert H. Humphrey School of Public Affairs. These courses introduced him to the similarities and the differences between management in government and in business. After graduating with his PhD, Schroeder joined the faculty of the University of Massachusetts School of Management, where, as part of his service, he worked with several state agencies on regional development. While at UMass he met Alan Robinson. The two began a decades-long collaboration that has resulted in the co-authoring of four books, including the bestselling *Ideas Are Free*, and many journal articles, including two that won Shingo Prizes for research. Their work together took them all over the world in search of organizations that unleashed the potential in the ideas of their front-line people.

Schroeder left UMass to become the Herbert and Agnes Schulz Professor of Management at Valparaiso University, where he taught strategic management, leadership, and the management of innovation and change. While at Valpo he started the College of Business's graduate programs, which offer both MBA and Master of Engineering Management degrees with a focus on values-based leadership. Schroeder has also taken short teaching assignments in Europe and Asia.

Schroeder has published over a hundred articles, ranging from pieces in top academic journals such as the *Academy of Management Journal* and the *Strategic Management Journal,* to more practical articles in publications that include the *Wall Street Journal,* the *Journal of Government Financial Management,* and the *MIT Sloan Management Review.*

Schroeder served for six years on the Board of Examiners of the Malcolm Baldrige National Quality Award, was on the board of the American Creativity Association, and has served on three corporate boards of directors, including his current role as Chairman of the Board for a mid-sized manufacturing firm. He has consulted with organizations on four continents, ranging in size from global giants including Siemens and NTT to family businesses and NGOs. One of his favorite consulting jobs was working with Subaru in its effort to help the National Parks become zero landfill.

Schroeder resides in the Chicago area and is a Senior Research Professor at Valparaiso University.

Berrett–Koehler
Publishers

Berrett-Koehler is an independent publisher dedicated to an ambitious mission: *Connecting people and ideas to create a world that works for all.*

Our publications span many formats, including print, digital, audio, and video. We also offer online resources, training, and gatherings. And we will continue expanding our products and services to advance our mission.

We believe that the solutions to the world's problems will come from all of us, working at all levels: in our society, in our organizations, and in our own lives. Our publications and resources offer pathways to creating a more just, equitable, and sustainable society. They help people make their organizations more humane, democratic, diverse, and effective (and we don't think there's any contradiction there). And they guide people in creating positive change in their own lives and aligning their personal practices with their aspirations for a better world.

And we strive to practice what we preach through what we call "The BK Way." At the core of this approach is *stewardship,* a deep sense of responsibility to administer the company for the benefit of all of our stakeholder groups, including authors, customers, employees, investors, service providers, sales partners, and the communities and environment around us. Everything we do is built around stewardship and our other core values of *quality, partnership, inclusion,* and *sustainability.*

This is why Berrett-Koehler is the first book publishing company to be both a B Corporation (a rigorous certification) and a benefit corporation (a for-profit legal status), which together require us to adhere to the highest standards for corporate, social, and environmental performance. And it is why we have instituted many pioneering practices (which you can learn about at www.bkconnection.com), including the Berrett-Koehler Constitution, the Bill of Rights and Responsibilities for BK Authors, and our unique Author Days.

We are grateful to our readers, authors, and other friends who are supporting our mission. We ask you to share with us examples of how BK publications and resources are making a difference in your lives, organizations, and communities at www.bkconnection.com/impact.

Dear reader,

Thank you for picking up this book and welcome to the worldwide BK community! You're joining a special group of people who have come together to create positive change in their lives, organizations, and communities.

What's BK all about?

Our mission is to connect people and ideas to create a world that works for all.

Why? Our communities, organizations, and lives get bogged down by old paradigms of self-interest, exclusion, hierarchy, and privilege. But we believe that can change. That's why we seek the leading experts on these challenges—and share their actionable ideas with you.

A welcome gift

To help you get started, we'd like to offer you a **free copy** of one of our bestselling ebooks:

www.bkconnection.com/welcome

When you claim your **free ebook**, you'll also be subscribed to our blog.

Our freshest insights

Access the best new tools and ideas for leaders at all levels on our blog at ideas.bkconnection.com.

Sincerely,

Your friends at Berrett-Koehler